Cathy ©1991. Cathy Guisewite. Reprinted with permission of Universal Press Syndicate.

The Newlywed Cookbook

Robin Walsh

The Newlywed Cookbook

Published by
R&E Publishers
P.O. Box 2008
Saratoga, CA 95070
(408) 866-6303
Fax: (408) 866-0825

I.S.B.N. 1-56875-093-5
L.C. 91-61310

Acknowledgments

I would like to thank all family and friends who encouraged me to pursue a dream.

To my husband, who sustained all my successes and failures and always inspired me to go on. Thank you for your continued strength and support, thus making this book possible.

To my mom and dad for their tireless support and willingness to sample endless creations. Your recommendations and constructive criticism helped make this book what it is.

To my close friends Karyn and Caroline, who provided daily advice and encouragement.

To all other family and friends who donated priceless recipes and suggestions throughout the development of this book.

And, to all newly married couples. Enjoy the magic and romance of marriage while nourishing your relationship with culinary delights. May you savor your first years together and build a bond that lasts a lifetime.

TABLE OF CONTENTS

The book will be set up in an A La Carte fashion. Food categories have been separated by chapter to ease decision making and location of the desired meal. Side dishes, desserts and treats to accompany the main dish are found in subsequent chapters. The exception is the Special Occasions chapter in which entire meals have been compiled based on harmony and balance of flavors and colors.

PREFACE

The following cookbook has been developed specifically for the newly married. It was developed during the early stages of my marriage, in an effort to benefit the inexperienced.

After several attempts at a decent meal, I came to the realization that there were probably hundreds of people like myself who yearned to create a fantastic meal for two, and after hours in the kitchen, ended up ordering out for pizza! On several occasions, while I was trying to create a romantic (and edible) dinner for my husband, I was disappointed to find that most cookbooks are written for the experienced cook. I spent most of the preparation time looking up things in the index, or a dictionary.

The recipes in this book were written using first hand experiences. I did all of the experimenting so you don't have to! Explicit directions are given to guide you through each recipe. If my purpose in writing this book is successful, you will become confident in your cooking ability and have a valuable resource to refer to for future cooking experiences. My hope is to encourage many would-be cooks to "test the waters" and learn to be creative on their own. In addition, this book guides you through several romantic meals for two, as well as fabulous meals for special occasions.

This book makes no assumptions on your cooking level, even the basics are covered. If you have already learned the basics of food preparation, this will be a refresher course.

You may recognize some of the recipes in this book. Recipes that are similar to dishes you grew up eating, with slight variations to give them a "boost". In addition, I have tried to break the monotony by throwing in a few unique and unusual dishes. If they sound a bit strange, try them anyway, you may be in for quite a surprise!

In many instances, I have suggested servings of 2-3 or 2-4. I have found that other cookbooks suggest serving sizes that are too small for hearty appetites. If you find that the servings are too large, you'll have great leftovers!

For your convenience, I have also included the preparation and cooking time for each recipe. After a long day of work, these guidelines should help make your meal making decision a bit easier.

POTS AND PANS

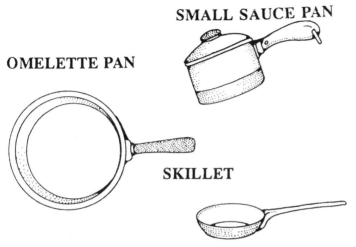

SMALL SAUCE PAN

OMELETTE PAN

SKILLET

LOW OR SMALL SAUCE PAN - probably the most used pan in the kitchen. Used for cooking vegetables, poaching in very little water, sauteing, simmering and for making sauces.

FLARE-SIDED SAUCE PAN - used for heating milk, soup, and when a reduction in liquid is necessary (the wide surface area aids in rapid evaporation)

SAUCEPOT OR STOCKPOT - used for cooking large quantities of vegetables, pasta, making stock, soups and stews

LARGE STOCKPOT - mainly used for large quantities of food, making stocks and soups, pasta, cooking larger items such as ears of corn, artichokes and lobster

SAUTE PAN - higher sides than a skillet, mainly used for browning meats and poultry, stir-frying, browning onions, garlic and vegetables

SKILLET - frying pan with sides that slope outward. Used for frying meat, poultry and vegetables over high heat.

OMELETTE PAN - flatter and smaller than a skillet. Curved sides to aid in rolling the egg around the pan.

CHICKEN FRYER - deep frying pan with a lid. Used for browning chicken and then steaming under cover. Useful in any dish where browning is followed by braising.

DEEP FAT FRYER - pot with wide surface area. Contains wire mesh basket and fits inside and is used as a strainer.

VEGETABLE STEAMER - large stock pot with an inner perforated pot or wire basket for holding vegetables and straining

BLANCHING POT - similar to vegetable steamer, however inner pot is perforated on all sides, like a colander. Inner pot is used for immersing vegetables quickly into rapidly boiling water and removing and draining all at once.

PAELLA PAN - Spanish pan used for cooking Paella, a rice-based dish

DOUBLE BOILER - two pots, one set inside the other. Simmering water in the lower pot while food cooks in the upper pot prevents burning or overheating delicate foods (i.e., chocolate, custard)

PRESSURE COOKER - used for cooking food under the pressure of steam

WOK - either conventional range top or electric. Used for stir-frying a variety of meat, poultry, seafood and vegetables

CASSEROLE DISHES - designed for slow cooking in the oven. Range in size from 1 pint to 8 quarts.

DUTCH OVEN - covered stock pot usually used for beef stew or pot roast

ROASTING PAN - used for roasting meat and poultry, can be used to hold custard cups

BAKING OR COOKIE SHEET - used for cookies, breads, pastries, rolls

JELLYROLL PAN - baking sheet with small edges, used for jellyrolls, brownies

CAKE PAN (round or square) - round pans available in 8" or 9" diameters usually used for layered cakes; square pans usually 8" in diameter and used for unlayered, unfilled cakes or bars

SPRINGFORM PAN - a high sided cake pan that is made up of two pieces, the sides unlatch from the bottom. Used for tortes, cheesecakes, and dishes that are otherwise difficult to remove from a pan.

BUNDT PAN - usually used to make pound or other dense cakes. The tube in the middle is used to promote even baking.

TUBE PAN - high sided baking pan usually used for cakes such as angel food. The tube in the middle promotes even baking and helps aid in rapid rising.

RING MOLD - many uses include; cakes, breads, gelatin molds, rice rings

PIE PAN - range in size for 8-10 inches in diameter and 1 to 1 1/4 inches deep

QUICHE OR TART PAN - low fluted sides with or without a removable bottom. Range in size from 8-12 inches for a quiche pan and generally 4 inches for a tart pan.

MUFFIN TIN - used for muffins and cupcakes. Pans range in size from holding 6-12 regular size muffins, to 24 tiny muffins.

BREAD PAN - regular bread size is 9 x 5 x 3. Smaller bread pans are 8 1/2 x 4 1/2 x 2 1/2 and are generally used for quick breads. Miniature bread pans are also available.

CAKE PAN

DOUBLE BOILER

QUICHE OR TART PAN

Pizza & Pasta

PERSONAL PIZZA

20-30 minutes to prepare   *1+ hour to rise*   *18-20 minutes to bake*

Everyone loves pizza. It comes in so many shapes, sizes and flavors that it's hard not to please even the most finicky palate. This recipe is basic, a starting tool to be worked with. Any and all of your favorite toppings can be used with this fabulous dough recipe. You may not find the time to make pizza after work, but some weekend, when you have an extra hour—it's worth the wait!

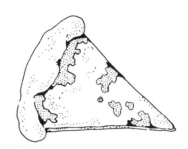

1	package active dry yeast	2	teaspoons olive or vegetable oil
1	cup warm water	2 1/2 - 3	cups all-purpose flour
	(feels warm on inside of wrist)	1/2	teaspoon salt

Topping:

28 oz. can peeled Italian plum tomatoes, drained and chopped (allow most of the seeds to fall out)
8 oz. Mozzarella cheese, grated   1/8   cup Parmesan cheese

Topping of your choice, i.e., pepperoni, cooked sausage or ground beef, broccoli, mushrooms, green peppers, onions, black olives, anchovies.

Dissolve yeast in warm water and let stand for 5 minutes. Add salt, olive oil and 2 1/2 cups of the flour. If you have a mixer with a dough hook attachment, or a food processor, blend until smooth and elastic. If you do not, blend with a fork or wooden spoon. If dough is sticky, add remaining flour, a little at a time until a manageable dough forms. Knead for 5 minutes on the appropriate speed with your mixer or food processor, or turn to a lightly floured surface and knead for 10 minutes, no less. Place dough in a large, lightly oiled bowl and turn to coat all sides with the oil. Cover with a cloth or dish towel and let rise in a warm place, free from draft until doubled in bulk, about 1 hour. Preheat oven to 450 degrees. Brush a 14" pizza pan with oil or cooking spray (if you don't have a pizza pan, use a baking sheet). Punch dough down with your fist and remove from bowl. Place dough in the middle of the pan or baking sheet and with the heal of your hand, press dough out until it reaches the edges of the pan (or forms a 12-14" circle). When using a pizza pan, continue pressing dough down to form a 1" lip up the sides. For a thick crust, let sit for 20 minutes, to rise. For a thinner, crispy crust, fill right away. Cover dough with an even layer of Mozzarella cheese. Top with chopped tomatoes. Place the topping(s) of your choice on top of the tomatoes and sprinkle with Parmesan cheese. Bake for 18-20 minutes, or until cheese is melted and edges are golden. Serve immediately.

MAKES 1 14" PIZZA (ABOUT 8 SLICES)

DOLLIE'S MICROWAVE LASAGNA WITH SPINACH

10-15 minutes to prepare   *40 minutes to cook*

This recipe is a super-easy dish that tastes like it took all day to prepare. I use spinach in this recipe, however, your favorite vegetable may be substituted, (i.e., broccoli, mushrooms, asparagus tips, zucchini)—or you can skip the vegetables altogether.

1/2	box lasagna noodles	1	egg, optional
8 oz.	Mozzarella cheese, grated	1	box frozen spinach, thawed and drained
8 oz.	Ricotta cheese	48 oz.	jar of spaghetti sauce
1/2	cup cottage cheese	1/4	cup Parmesan cheese

In a large bowl, combine 1/2 of the Mozzarella cheese, all of the Ricotta, cottage cheese, egg and spinach. Mix well.

In an 8 x 12 x 2 glass or microwave safe dish, pour in enough spaghetti sauce to cover the bottom. Place three UNCOOKED noodles, side by side on top of sauce (place 2-3 side by side, whatever fits in your baking dish). Put 1/3 of cheese mixture on top of noodles and add more spaghetti sauce. Cover with three more noodles and half of remaining cheese mixture. Top with more noodles and repeat procedure. (ORDER: noodles/cheese/sauce—noodles/cheese/sauce—noodles/cheese/sauce—noodles) Spread enough sauce on top to cover the noodles. Top with remaining Mozzarella and Parmesan cheese.

Cover with plastic wrap and microwave on HIGH for 5 minutes. Continue cooking on 1/2 (50%) power for 35 minutes, turning every 10 minutes. Cool at least 10 minutes before serving.

SERVES 2-4

NOTE: This recipe can easily be turned into a vegetable lasagna by adding a layer of vegetables on top of the cheese mixture in each layer. Vegetables I recommend using include zucchini, fresh broccoli, carrots, onions, mushrooms and eggplant.

LINGUINE WITH VEGETABLES

20-25 minutes to prepare

This recipe is a take-off on pasta primavera. The most appealing aspect of this dish is that you can create it however you like it best, using your favorite veggies. If you don't like the vegetables I have chosen, substitute your own. In fact, if you have leftover chicken, it becomes quite tasty in this medley of vegetables, cheese and pasta.

1/2 lb. linguine	3 tablespoons butter or margarine
1 small onion, chopped	2 tablespoons flour
1/2 lb. mushrooms, sliced	1 cup milk
2 carrots, sliced diagonally into bite size pieces	1 packed cup grated Cheddar or Swiss cheese
1 cup broccoli, cut into small pieces	1 teaspoon Dijon mustard
1 red pepper, cut into bite size pieces	1 tablespoon fresh parsley
	Salt and black pepper to taste

Cook linguine according to package directions, drain and set aside. In a large pot of boiling water, blanche the carrots, broccoli, and red pepper for 2 minutes, until tender crisp. In a medium sauce pan, melt 1 tablespoon of the butter over medium heat and add the onion and mushrooms. Saute until tender, about 3-5 minutes. Remove from pan and set aside. In the same pan, melt the remaining butter, and gradually add the flour. Mix with a wire whisk until mixture is smooth. Gradually add milk, stirring constantly with a whisk. When mixture is slightly thickened, add cheese, mustard and parsley and mix well. Stir in onion, mushrooms and blanched vegetables and toss gently. Season with salt and pepper, spoon over pasta and serve.

SERVES 2

LINGUINE WITH FRESH TOMATO SAUCE

25-30 minutes preparation and cooking time

The tomato sauce in this recipe is light and refreshing. It's a nice change from the store-bought, salty varieties. The sauce can be prepared in advance and refrigerated or frozen until ready to use. Reheat in sauce pan over medium-low heat and serve over cooked pasta.

1/2 lb. linguine	1/2 teaspoon ground black pepper
6 large ripe tomatoes	1/4 teaspoon oregano
1-2 cloves garlic, minced	1/4 cup fresh basil, minced
1/8 cup olive oil	Parmesan cheese for topping
1/2 teaspoon salt	

Bring a large pot of water to a boil. With a sharp knife, make a large X on the bottom of each tomato. Stab the top of each tomato with a fork and plunge into boiling water for 10 seconds and remove. Cool slightly, and peel off skin. Core each tomato, cut into 8 slices and remove seeds with a small spoon. Cook linguine according to package directions, drain, run under cold water to prevent further cooking, drain and set aside. In a medium sauce pan, combine the tomatoes, garlic, oil, salt, pepper and oregano. Simmer over low heat for 5 minutes, add basil and cook for an additional 5 minutes, until heated through. Pour tomato sauce over linguine and serve with grated Parmesan cheese on the side.

SERVES 2

FETTUCINE THROUGH THE GARDEN

20 minutes to prepare   *20-25 minutes to bake*

This dish was created by my friend Steve when he was looking for a good meal FAST. It's a unique combination of flavors and it enables you to create a fabulous meal in less than an hour.

1/2	lb. fettucine noodles	1/2	cup grated Parmesan cheese
1-2	tablespoons butter or margarine	1	cup heavy cream
1	can minced clams	1/4	cup parsley, minced
1-2	cloves garlic, minced	2	cups broccoli florets
1/2	cup grated Romano cheese		Salt and black pepper to taste

Preheat oven to 350 degrees. Blanche broccoli in a large pot of boiling water for 1 minute. Drain, rinse under cold water and set aside. Cook fettucine according to package directions. While the pasta cooks, heat butter in a large skillet over medium heat. Add minced clams and saute for 5 minutes, stirring occasionally. Stir in garlic and saute for 2 minutes. Drain fettucine and rinse under water. In a large bowl, combine fettucine, clams, cheeses, cream and parsley. Mix well. Place broccoli in the bottom of a 2 quart casserole dish. Pour fettucine mixture on top, cover and bake for 20-25 minutes, or until heated through. Serve warm.

SERVES 2-3

SPAGHETTI WITH ZUCCHINI CREAM SAUCE

20-30 minutes preparation and cooking time

This recipe is a delightfully creamy pasta dish that's not too heavy. The combination of zucchini, lemon and cream creates a flavorful, light meal in minutes.

2 shallots, minced	1/2 teaspoon salt
1 clove garlic, whole	1/4 teaspoon ground black pepper
1 cup heavy cream	2 tablespoons fresh parsley, chopped
1 whole lemon	1/2 lb. spaghetti
1 large zucchini, cut julienne style	Parmesan cheese
1/2 cup Ricotta cheese	
1/2 cup cottage cheese	

Cook pasta according to package directions, drain and set aside. (To prevent pasta from sticking together, stir in about 1/4 cup of the cream before using it in the sauce.) Combine shallots, garlic and cream in a medium sauce pan. Simmer over medium high heat for 10-12 minutes, making sure mixture does not boil. In a food processor fitted with a metal blade, or in the blender, process the Ricotta and cottage cheeses until smooth and creamy. Remove garlic clove from cream mixture and discard. Fold cheeses into cream mixture and heat through. Add zucchini, 1 tablespoon of grated lemon rind, salt and pepper. Simmer over medium heat until zucchini is tender, about 8-10 minutes. Stir in parsley and 1 teaspoon fresh lemon juice. Mix well and serve over spaghetti. Serve with grated Parmesan cheese on the side.

SERVES 2

HAM, CHEESE AND NOODLE CASSEROLE

15-20 minutes to prepare

30 minutes to bake

Another dish from my friend Steve. This dish incorporates the dynamic flavors of ham, tomatoes, pasta and cheese. The dish is done in layers creating an ensemble that boasts a slightly spicy flavor. Takes just minutes to prepare too!

8 oz.	package egg noodles	2	tablespoons fresh parsley, minced
1	tablespoon butter or margarine	1/2	teaspoon black pepper
1	small onion, chopped	1/2 lb.	ham, sliced into chunks
1-2	cloves garlic, minced	8 oz.	Mozzarella cheese, grated
29 oz.	can tomato sauce		
1/2	teaspoon oregano		
2	teaspoons fresh basil, minced, or 1 teaspoon dried		

Preheat oven to 350 degrees. Cook egg noodles according to package directions using the minimum suggested cooking time, drain and set aside. In small sauce pan heat butter over medium heat and add onion and garlic. Saute until tender. Stir in tomato sauce, oregano, basil, parsley and pepper. Simmer until heated through. Remove from heat and pour 1/3 of mixture into the bottom of a 2 quart casserole dish. Place 1/2 of noodles on top. Cover the noodles with 1/2 of the ham followed by 1/3 of the Mozzarella cheese. Repeat procedure, sauce/noodles/ham/cheese. Cover with remaining sauce and top with remaining cheese. Cover with lid or foil and bake for 25 minutes. Remove lid and bake for an additional 5 minutes. Serve hot.

SERVES 2-4

EGGPLANT CASSEROLE

20 minutes to prepare   *45 minutes to bake*

This variation of eggplant parmesan is packed with flavor and makes great leftovers (if there are any).

8 oz.	package pasta noodles, (i.e., spirals, twists)	2	Italian plum tomatoes, chopped
1	medium eggplant	8 oz.	can tomato sauce
1-2	eggs, slightly beaten	4 oz.	can tomato paste
1/2	cup bread crumbs	1/2	teaspoon oregano
2	tablespoons butter or margarine	1/2	teaspoon dried basil
1	small onion, chopped	1/4	teaspoon black pepper
1	medium green bell pepper, chopped	1/4	cup grated Mozzarella cheese

In a small sauce pan combine onion, green pepper, plum tomatoes, tomato sauce, tomato paste, oregano, basil and pepper. Mix well and simmer over medium heat. Continue simmering sauce while preparing the rest of the dish. Preheat oven to 350 degrees. Cook pasta according to package directions using the minimum suggested cooking time, drain and set aside. Peel eggplant, slice in half lengthwise and cut into 1/4" thick slices. Dip eggplant into eggs and then into bread crumbs, turning to coat both sides. Melt butter in a large skillet over medium high heat. Saute eggplant in butter until golden brown on both sides. Remove from skillet and place half of the sauteed eggplant in the bottom of a lightly greased 2 quart casserole dish. Top with half of the cooked pasta. Cover with 1/2 of the tomato sauce. Place second half of eggplant evenly on top of sauce, cover with remaining pasta and then remaining sauce. Sprinkle grated Mozzarella cheese on top, cover and bake for 30 minutes. Uncover and bake for 15 minutes. Serve hot.

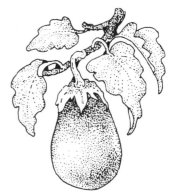

BROCCOLI, CAULIFLOWER, AND ORZO CASSEROLE

20 minutes to prepare   *30 minutes to bake*

This is a simple dish that tastes fabulous. Orzo is a unique pasta, and it spruces up this cheesy, vegetable dish.

8 oz. **(1 1/4 cups) uncooked Orzo (pasta that looks like rice)**

1 cup cauliflower florets	**1 cup milk**
1 cup broccoli florets	**2 eggs, slightly beaten**
1 teaspoon olive or vegetable oil	**1 cup sharp Cheddar cheese, grated**
1/4 cup onion, chopped	**1/2 teaspoon salt**
1 ripe tomato, chopped	**1/4 teaspoon pepper**
1 teaspoon fresh parsley, chopped or 1/2 teaspoon dried	

Preheat oven to 375 degrees. Cook Orzo according package directions, drain and set aside. Bring a large pot of water to a boil and blanche cauliflower and broccoli for 1-2 minutes, until tender crisp. In a small skillet, saute the onion in oil until tender. Combine Orzo, cauliflower, broccoli, onion, tomato and remaining ingredients in 2 quart casserole dish and mix well. Cover and bake for 30-35 minutes, or until set. Cool slightly before serving.

SERVES 2-3

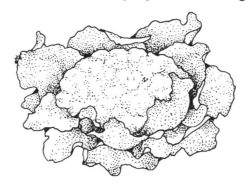

HOME-MADE CHEESE RAVIOLI

30-35 minutes to prepare   *15-20 minutes to cook*

One day I decided to get courageous and make my own ravioli. Much to my surprise, it was simple to prepare and tasted far better than the pre-made variety. Some lazy Sunday afternoon, when you have a little extra time, experiment with the following recipe. You will be pleasantly surprised and thoroughly enjoy the results. If you truly don't have the time, but you want home-made ravioli, use Won Ton wrappers instead of making the pasta. Won Ton wrappers can be found in the produce section of most supermarkets.

Pasta:

| 3 1/2 cups all-purpose flour | 4 tablespoons milk |
| 3 eggs | 2 tablespoons olive or vegetable oil |

Filling:

Combine the following ingredients in a large bowl and mix well.

15 oz. Ricotta cheese

1 egg	Pinch of salt
1 tablespoon fresh parsley, or 1 1/2 teaspoons dried	Pinch of black pepper
1/4 cup grated Parmesan cheese	Dash of nutmeg (optional)

Combine all pasta ingredients in a large bowl or food processor fitted with the metal blade. Blend with a wooden spoon or process until mixture is smooth, firm and dry. If pasta is too moist, add more flour as necessary. If you have a pasta machine or pasta attachment, follow the directions for ravioli. If not, turn to a lightly floured surface and knead for 10 minutes, sprinkling the work surface with flour and kneading until dough is smooth and consistent. Split dough in half and roll out with a rolling pin until 1/8" thick. Cut dough into two large, fairly equal squares (use a ruler if you have to). On one of the halves, spread the filling out evenly. Place the second half on top and with a pastry cutter or square cookie cutter, cut into 2" squares. If necessary, seal each square by pressing down the edges with a fork. Cook ravioli in a large pot of rapidly boiling water for 15-20 minutes. Drain, and serve alone or with sauce and grated cheese.

SERVES 2-4

BAKED ZITI

10-15 minutes to prepare   *35 minutes to bake*

This dish requires little effort, yet it's a perfect meal for entertaining. Everything (but the final baking) can be prepared in advance and refrigerated. Once your guests arrive, you just bake and serve!

8   oz. package ziti noodles
15   oz. jar of spaghetti sauce
8   oz. Ricotta or cottage cheese
8   oz. Mozzarella cheese

Preheat oven to 350 degrees. (If you plan to make this meal ahead, prepare everything as directed and refrigerate. Bake according to directions when ready to serve.) Cook ziti according to package directions, using the minimum suggested cooking time, drain and set aside. Pour enough spaghetti sauce into the bottom of a 2 quart casserole dish to cover the bottom. In a small bowl, combine Ricotta cheese and 2/3 of the Mozzarella cheese. Place a layer of ziti noodles on top of the sauce in the casserole. Cover with half of the cheese mixture, and then more sauce. Repeat procedure, noodles, cheese, sauce and top with remaining Mozzarella cheese. Cover and bake for 30 minutes. Uncover and bake for an additional 5 minutes. Cool slightly before serving.

SERVES 3-4*

*This recipe can easily be doubled and tripled for a large number of people.

2

Chicken

KITCHEN SINK CHICKEN

10 minutes to prepare   *1 hour to bake*

The perfect meal to create when you have a refrigerator full of leftovers. Use up vegetables, fruits, cheeses, etc. Just throw whatever you have on top of the chicken and bake according to directions. This recipe is a great starter for many future experiments.

1	whole chicken breast, halved, (with or without skin)		
1	cup seasoned wild rice	1	large tomato, chopped*
1	small onion, chopped	6-8	fresh mushrooms, sliced*
2	cups chicken broth		Salt and black pepper to taste

Preheat oven to 350 degrees. Wash chicken and remove excess fat. Season both sides with salt and pepper and place in the bottom of a shallow baking dish. Spread the uncooked rice around the chicken pieces. Spread tomato, onion and mushrooms evenly on top and around chicken (plus whatever leftovers you have). Pour chicken broth over everything, cover with foil and bake for 1 hour, or until chicken is tender and cooked through and rice has absorbed all liquid. Serve.

SERVES 2

*If desired, substitute your leftovers for these ingredients.

TARRAGON CHICKEN WITH PEPPER CREAM SAUCE

20 minutes to prepare   *35-40 minutes to cook*

This creamy chicken dish prepared with tarragon is ideal for all occasions.
Entertaining or not, it's a perfect meal.

1	whole, boneless chicken breast, halved and without skin		
2	tablespoons butter or margarine	10-12	mushrooms, sliced
1	shallot, chopped	1/2	teaspoon salt
1	cup chicken broth	6	black peppercorns
1/4	cup brandy	1	cup light cream
1	cup dry white wine	1	tablespoon all-purpose flour
1/4	cup chopped fresh tarragon or 2 teaspoons dried		

TARRAGON

In a large sauce pan melt the butter over medium heat. Wash chicken and remove any fat. Saute chicken in butter until golden brown on both sides and remove from pan. In the same pan, add chicken broth and shallot. Simmer until shallot is tender, about 5 minutes. Return chicken to pan and add brandy, wine, tarragon, salt and peppercorns. Bring to a boil, cover, reduce heat and simmer for 30 minutes. Remove chicken, place on serving plate and keep warm. Strain liquid mixture to remove peppercorns, and return liquid to pan. Add mushrooms and simmer for 5 minutes. In a small bowl combine the cream and flour and mix well with a whisk. Gradually stir mixture into mushroom sauce and mix well. (If sauce seems too thick, add more wine.) Pour sauce over chicken pieces and serve.

SERVES 2-3

NOTE: Serve with rice, pasta or potatoes on the side.

DIJON CHICKEN WITH MUSHROOMS

40 minutes preparation and cooking time

The ingredients in this dish may surprise you. However, the combination creates a meal that is deliciously light and conveniently low in fat and calories.

1	whole, boneless chicken breast, halved and without skin
	Flour for dredging
1-2	tablespoons butter or margarine
1	cup chicken broth
1	cup dry white wine
1	small onion, sliced
10-12	fresh mushrooms, sliced

Juice of one whole lemon
10 whole black peppercorns
6 sprigs fresh thyme, or 1 teaspoon dried
1 tablespoon honey
1 tablespoon Dijon mustard

Melt butter in large skillet over medium high heat. Dredge chicken breast halves in flour and coat well. Saute in chicken in butter until golden, remove from pan and set aside. To the same skillet, add chicken broth, wine, onion, lemon juice, peppercorns and thyme and bring to a boil. Reduce heat, cover and simmer for 10 minutes. Strain liquid through a fine sieve or strainer, discard the onion and peppercorns and return liquid to pan. Stir in honey, mustard and mushrooms and bring to a boil. Reduce heat and simmer for 10 minutes. Add chicken to pan and simmer until cooked through and mixture has thickened, about 15 minutes. Serve chicken with sauce on the side or on top. (I suggest serving this dish with rice or pasta to soak up the extra, delicious sauce.)

SERVES 2

CHICKEN MARSALA

30-40 minutes preparation and cooking time

Simmering chicken in Marsala wine and mushrooms creates a tender, flavorful chicken dish with an extremely enticing aroma. I suggest serving the chicken with rice or pasta on the side to soak up the precious sauce.

1	whole, boneless chicken breast, halved and without skin		
1	tablespoon butter or margarine	3/4	cup Monteray Jack cheese, grated
1	cup beef broth	1	tablespoon cornstarch
1/2	cup Marsala wine	1/2	cup water
8-10	fresh mushrooms, sliced		

In a large skillet, saute the mushrooms in butter over medium heat until tender and releasing juice. Remove from skillet and set aside. Add the chicken to the skillet and saute over medium high heat until golden brown on both sides. Add beef broth, Marsala wine and mushrooms. Simmer for 20-25 minutes, or until chicken is tender. Preheat oven to 250 degrees. Remove chicken from skillet and place on an oven-safe plate. Sprinkle the top of each piece with grated cheese and place in oven to keep warm. Dissolve cornstarch in water and add to skillet. Stir until mixture thickens, about 5 minutes. Pour sauce over chicken and serve.

SERVES 2

CHICKEN IN MUSHROOM-SHERRY SAUCE

35-40 minutes preparation and cooking time

This chicken dish is complimented by a rich wild mushroom-sherry sauce. The sauce is delicious so serve this meal with lots of rice, pasta or bread on the side to absorb any extra.

- 1 **whole, boneless chicken breast, halved and without skin**
- 2 **tablespoons butter or margarine**
- 1 oz **dried porcini or shitake mushrooms**
- 1/8 **teaspoon ground black pepper**

- 3/4 **cup Sherry (Sherry Cooking Wine is fine)**
- 1 **teaspoon chopped fresh thyme, or 1/2 teaspoon dried**
- 1 **cup heavy cream**

Soak dried mushrooms in 1/2 cup warm water for 15-20 minutes. Strain mushrooms through a paper towel-lined colander, reserving the juice. Rinse mushrooms under water to remove any grit, slice into bite size pieces and set aside. Heat butter in a large skillet over medium heat. Add chicken and saute until golden brown on both sides. Add mushrooms and mushroom juice to the skillet. Combine pepper, 1/2 cup of Sherry and thyme and add to skillet. Bring mixture to a boil, reduce heat, cover and simmer until chicken is tender, about 15 minutes. Remove chicken and mushrooms from skillet with a slotted spoon, reserving juice in pan. Set aside and keep warm. Add remaining Sherry to skillet and simmer over medium high heat until liquid is reduced by half, stirring constantly. Reduce heat and add cream. Simmer, stirring constantly until liquid is reduced by half and sauce has a gravy-like consistency. Pour sauce over chicken and mushrooms and serve.

SERVES 2

HAWAIIAN CHICKEN

10 minutes to prepare   *30-35 minutes to bake*

The combination of sweet and sour ingredients in this dish, create a meal so authentic that you can almost feel the tropical breeze and smell the salt in the air!

1	whole, boneless chicken breast, halved and without skin		
1	tablespoon butter or margarine	1/2	cup apricot preserves
1	can crushed pineapple	1	tablespoon soy sauce

Preheat oven to 350 degrees. In a small sauce pan combine the pineapple, apricot preserves and soy sauce. Simmer over low heat while you cook the chicken, stirring occasionally. Melt butter in a large skillet and add chicken. Saute over medium high heat until golden brown on both sides. Remove from pan and place in a shallow baking dish. Spoon pineapple mixture evenly over chicken and bake for 30-35 minutes, or until chicken is tender and cooked through. Serve warm.

SERVES 2

KARYN'S SESAME CHICKEN WITH APRICOT DIPPING SAUCE

15-20 minutes to prepare   *30 minutes to bake*

This dish is fun to serve when you're looking for something different. The sesame seeds add a surprising crunch to the chicken, while the dipping sauce boasts a sweet and sour flavor. This tasty combination is sure to please everyone's palate. (Make sure you make enough—there are seldom any leftovers!)

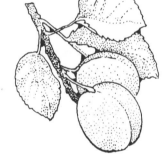

1 1/2	**lbs. skinned, boneless chicken breasts**
1	**cup bread crumbs**
1/4	**cup sesame seeds**
2	**eggs, slightly beaten**
2-3	**tablespoons butter or margarine**
1	**cup apricot preserves**
1/4	**cup soy sauce**
1/4	**teaspoon black pepper**

Preheat oven to 350 degrees. Combine bread crumbs and sesame seeds in a medium size bowl and set aside. Wash chicken and cut into finger-size strips. Dip chicken into eggs and then into bread crumb mixture, turning to coat all sides. In a large skillet, melt the butter until bubbly and add several pieces of chicken. Saute until golden brown on all sides. Place on baking sheet covered with foil. When all chicken has been sauteed, bake in oven for 25-30 minutes or until tender.

In a small sauce pan, combine the apricot preserves, soy sauce and pepper. Simmer over low heat until heated through (this mixture can simmer while the chicken cooks).

Serve chicken pieces with sauce on the side for dipping.

SERVES 2-3

KEVIN'S BARBECUED CHICKEN

30-40 minutes preparation and cooking time

This is, by far, the best barbecued chicken recipe you will ever taste. You'll be surprised to find that the chicken is boiled in the barbecue sauce before it is grilled. This method allows the chicken to absorb all the fabulous flavors, and prevents it from becoming dry, as it so often does on the grill.

2 lbs.	chicken pieces, with or without skin	3	tablespoons curry powder
1	large bottle of your favorite barbecue sauce	2	tablespoons chili powder
3/4	cup honey	1	tablespoon ground ginger
1/4	cup Worcestershire sauce	1	tablespoon cayenne pepper (optional)

Wash chicken pieces and set aside. Combine all remaining ingredients in a large sauce pan or stock pot. Add chicken and enough water to cover chicken with sauce. Bring mixture to a boil over high heat. Reduce heat and simmer chicken until cooked through and tender, about 12-15 minutes. Preheat outdoor grill. Remove chicken from sauce and set aside. Simmer remaining barbecue sauce, uncovered, until thoroughly reduced. When the sauce has reached a thick consistency, remove from heat and use to baste chicken on grill. Grill chicken until crispy on the outside and tender on the inside, basting frequently with the sauce. Serve.

SERVES 3-4

TOM'S BUFFALO STYLE CHICKEN WINGS

25-30 minutes preparation and cooking time

Chicken wings are the perfect fun-food for everyone. This is my husband's favorite and perfected recipe, a true Buffalo-style treat. When you make these wings, be sure you have plenty of napkins on hand. Serve with blue cheese salad dressing for dipping, and celery stalks to cool the wonderful fire that's ablaze in your mouth!*

2	lbs. chicken wings	8 oz.	tomato paste
1	tablespoon water	3	tablespoons butter, melted
1/3	cup hot sauce (i.e., cayenne pepper sauce)	1	tablespoon Tabasco sauce
2	packed tablespoons brown sugar	1/4	teaspoon ground black pepper
	Vegetable oil for frying, about 6 cups		

Wash chicken wings, cut off wing tips and split in half at the joints. In a large bowl, combine the tomato paste, water, butter, hot sauce, Tabasco sauce, brown sugar and pepper. Mix well with a wire whisk and set aside. Heat oil in a large sauce pan or deep fryer until approximately 375 degrees. Oil is ready to use when a small bread cube dropped in floats to the top and browns in about 1 minute. Drop a portion of the wings in the oil with a pair of tongs and fry until golden and cooked through (they will usually float to the top when done), about 5 minutes. Remove wings from oil and drop into tomato mixture. Stir to coat wings with sauce. Cook second batch of wings once oil has returned to the appropriate temperature. Continue cooking wings until all are done and drenched in sauce. Serve with a BIG glass of ice water!

SERVES 2-3

*NOTE 1: If you don't like your wings VERY spicy, reduce the amount of hot sauce and Tabasco sauce for a more mild version.

NOTE 2: Homemade blue cheese dressing is easy to prepare; combine 1/3 cup sour cream with 1/4 cup of crumbled up blue cheese and mix well.

STIR-FRIED CHICKEN WITH VEGETABLES

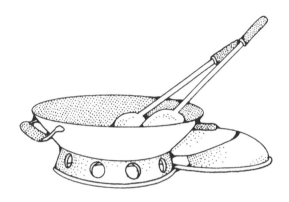

30 minutes preparation and cooking time

Stir frying chicken and vegetables is a quick and easy way to prepare a delicious meal. If you don't own a wok, use a large skillet instead (and buy one soon, you won't regret it!)

1 lb.	boneless chicken breasts, skinned	1	cup fresh mushrooms, sliced
1	tablespoon olive oil	1	cup snow peas, ends trimmed
1	small onion, chopped	1/4	cup Marsala wine
1	clove garlic, minced	1/8	cup soy sauce
1	green pepper, cut into thin strips	1	tablespoon corn starch
1	carrot, sliced diagonally into bite size pieces	1/2	cup water
1	cup broccoli, cut into small pieces		

Wash the chicken and cut into bite size pieces. In a wok, or a large skillet, combine the olive oil, onion and garlic and cook over medium heat until tender. Stir in chicken and saute for 2-3 minutes. Add all remaining ingredients, except the corn starch and water, and cook over medium-high heat until chicken is cooked through and vegetables are tender crisp, about 6-8 minutes, stirring frequently. Just before serving, dissolve corn starch in water and add to wok. Stir until sauce thickens. Serve over rice.

SERVES 2

SPICY CHICKEN AND RICE

10 minutes to prepare   *30 minutes to marinate   25-50 minutes to cook (depending on rice)*

This chicken and vegetable dish has a bit of a zing. Hot sauce is added, (you decide the quantity) to give it that extra boost!

1 whole boneless chicken breast, skinned and cut into bite size pieces	
1/4 cup red wine vinegar	1 medium green pepper, chopped
1/2 teaspoon thyme	1 medium red pepper, chopped
1/2 teaspoon oregano	2 cups chicken broth
1 (+ or -) teaspoon Tabasco or other hot sauce	
1 small onion, chopped	1 cup white or brown rice, uncooked
1 tablespoon olive or vegetable oil	Salt and black pepper to taste

In a large bowl, combine the chicken, vinegar, thyme, oregano and hot sauce. Toss to coat chicken with the marinade and set aside at room temperature for at least 30 minutes. Heat oil in a wok or large skillet. Add onion and saute until tender, about 3-5 minutes. Add chicken and marinade mixture and simmer until chicken is cooked through and most of the liquid has cooked off. Add red and green peppers, chicken broth and rice and mix well. Cover and simmer over medium heat until vegetables are tender and rice has absorbed liquid, about 20 minutes for white rice and 40 minutes for brown, stirring occasionally. Season with salt and pepper and serve.

SERVES 2-3

CHICKEN FAJITAS

20-25 minutes preparation and cooking time

I discovered this dish on my honeymoon, and made it my goal to create a similar dish. Fajitas are a fun, eat with your fingers, type meal that liven up any dinner table. It's fun to invite guests over to enjoy this messy meal where everyone assembles their own fajita. (I use chicken in this recipe, however you can use beef strips or shrimp—it tastes just as good!)

1   whole, boneless chicken breast, skinned and cut into strips

2 green peppers, cut into strips	**1 package tortillas**
1 large onion, sliced	**(use 6-8 flour or corn tortillas)**
2 medium tomatoes, chopped	**Sour cream**
Tabasco or other hot sauce	

Fajita Marinade:

1/4 cup soy sauce	**1 tablespoon corn syrup**
1/4 cup red wine vinegar	**1 tablespoon olive or vegetable oil**
1/4 teaspoon black pepper	

Combine all marinade ingredients in a large bowl and mix well. Add chicken strips to marinade and set aside while you cut up the vegetables. In a large skillet, saute chicken in marinade over medium heat until tender, about 5-7 minutes (to test doneness, slice one of the larger pieces in half). Steam the green pepper and onion, or simmer in a small amount of water until tender, but not wilted. Remove chicken from skillet, reserving marinade, and place on a serving platter, keep warm. Add onion and green pepper to skillet and simmer 2-3 minutes. Place on serving platter next to chicken. Warm tortillas according to package directions. Serve chicken and vegetables with warm tortillas, chopped tomatoes, Tabasco sauce and sour cream (if desired, serve with guacamole and refried beans for an authentic Mexican treat).

SERVES 2

CHICKEN CACCIATORE

15-20 minutes to prepare   *1 hour to cook*

Chicken Cacciatore has been a household favorite for many years. If you invite guests over for dinner, prepare this meal before they arrive and let it simmer during cocktails. While you enjoy your company, the chicken is getting acquainted with the other ingredients in the pot, and creating a savory meal on its own!

1   whole chicken breast, halved and without skin
1   cup fresh mushrooms, sliced   1/2   teaspoon curry powder
1   green pepper, chopped   1/4   teaspoon salt
1   medium onion, sliced   1/4   teaspoon pepper
1   tablespoon olive or vegetable oil   1/2   cup dry red wine
3   cups fresh tomatoes, chopped   1/2   cup chicken broth
1   teaspoon fresh basil, or 1/2 teaspoon dried
1   tablespoon chopped fresh parsley, or 1 1/2 teaspoons dried

In a large skillet, saute the mushrooms, green pepper and onion in oil until tender. Add chicken, tomatoes, basil, parsley, curry, salt, pepper, wine and broth. Cover and cook over medium-low heat until chicken is tender, about 45 minutes. Uncover and cook 15 more minutes. Serve over rice.

NOTE: If you DO decide to invite guests to dinner, I suggest increasing the ingredients somewhat; better to have too much than too little.

SERVES 2-3

LEMON CHICKEN

35-40 minutes preparation and cooking time

This is the perfect dish
for nights when you're
looking for something
light and easy. There are
no heavy cream sauces to
weigh you down, and the
preparation and cooking
requirements leave little
work on your part.

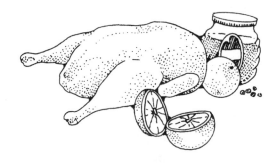

1	**whole chicken breast, halved and without skin**
	Salt and pepper to taste
	Paprika
2	**tablespoons butter or margarine**
1/4	**cup chopped onion**
6-8	**fresh mushrooms, sliced**
1	**lemon**
1/2	**cup dry white wine**

In a large skillet melt the butter over medium heat. Add onion and mushrooms and saute until
tender, about 3-5 minutes. Season both sides of chicken pieces with salt, pepper and paprika and
add to skillet. Saute until golden brown on both sides. Squeeze the juice of 1 whole lemon over
chicken, add wine, cover and simmer over medium heat for 20-30 minutes, until chicken is
tender, adding more wine if necessary to prevent sticking. Serve chicken with rice or pasta and
pour pan juices and mushrooms over top.

SERVES 2-3

CHICKEN TETRAZZINI

20-25 minutes to prepare   *20-25 minutes to bake*

Don't pass this one up!   This fabulous creation is so delicately cheesy, with hints of savory spices, you'll be making this dish more than once!

1	lb. boneless, skinned chicken pieces, cut into strips		
3-4	tablespoons butter or margarine	8-10	fresh mushrooms, sliced
1	small onion, chopped	2	tablespoons all-purpose flour
1/2	cup water	1/2	cup light or table cream
1/2	cup dry white wine	1/4	cup grated Parmesan cheese
1	tablespoon fresh parsley,	1/2	cup Mozzarella cheese, grated
	or 1 teaspoon dried	1/2	8 oz. package rainbow, tri-color macaroni
1/2	teaspoon dried thyme	1/4	cup bread crumbs
1/2	teaspoon salt	1/4	teaspoon black pepper

Preheat oven to 350 degrees. Cook pasta according to package directions, using the minimum suggested cooking time. Drain and pour into the bottom of a 2 quart casserole dish. In a large skillet, heat 1 tablespoon of butter and add onion. Saute until tender. Add chicken and saute over medium-high heat until golden brown on all sides. Add water, wine, parsley, thyme, salt and pepper. Cover and simmer over medium heat for 10-15 minutes, or until chicken is tender. While chicken cooks, heat mushrooms in a small skillet with 1 tablespoon butter until tender. Stir mushrooms into pasta. Remove chicken pieces from skillet with a slotted spoon and place evenly on top of the pasta and mushroom mixture. Strain and reserve remaining liquid from the pan to remove most of the onion, thyme and parsley, leaving the brown bits stuck to the bottom of the skillet. Melt 1-2 tablespoons of the butter in the skillet over medium heat and stir in the flour. Stir constantly with a wire whisk until mixture is smooth. Gradually add reserved liquid, stirring constantly and incorporating the brown bits from the bottom of the pan. When mixture thickens, gradually add the cream and then the cheeses. Pour cheese mixture over chicken and pasta. Top with an even layer of bread crumbs, cover and bake for 20-25 minutes or until heated through. Serve immediately.

SERVES 2-3

CHICKEN PARMESAN CASSEROLE

20-25 minutes to prepare   *40 minutes to bake*

This recipe has been developed to help make the preparation of chicken parmesan easier. This dish requires little effort on your part, and more effort on the part of the oven!

1	whole, boneless chicken breast, halved and without skin
1	egg, slightly beaten
1	cup dry bread crumbs
1	tablespoon fresh lemon juice
1-2	tablespoons butter or margarine
1/2	package (8 oz.) spaghetti or linguine
1/2	cup cottage cheese
4	oz. Mozzarella cheese, grated
1	medium size jar of spaghetti sauce, or:

8	oz. can tomato sauce	6	oz. can tomato paste
1/4	cup chopped onion	1/2	teaspoon oregano
1/2	teaspoon dried basil	Simmer all ingredients until onions are tender

Preheat oven to 350 degrees. Cook noodles according to package directions, using the minimum suggested cooking time, drain and place in the bottom of a 2 quart casserole dish. While the pasta is still warm, stir in cottage cheese with a fork. Wash chicken breasts and remove extra fat. Dip chicken into egg and then into bread crumbs, turning to coat both sides. Heat butter and lemon juice in a large skillet over medium-high heat. Add chicken and saute until golden brown on both sides. Remove from pan and place on top of noodles. Pour tomato sauce over chicken and noodles. Sprinkle Mozzarella cheese on top, cover and bake for 30 minutes. Uncover and bake for an additional 10 minutes, until cheese is melted. Cool slightly before serving.

SERVES 2

GREEN CHICKEN

25-30 minutes to prepare   *45 minutes to bake*

An interesting combination of spinach pasta, spinach and chicken. The ensemble creates a unique, tasty meal with lots of color.

		1	box frozen spinach, thawed and drained
2	cups cooked bite-size chicken pieces*	1	cup heavy cream
1	6-8 oz. package spinach pasta (it's green!)	1/2	teaspoon salt
1	tablespoon butter or margarine	1/4	teaspoon black pepper
1	small onion, chopped	1/4	cup bread crumbs
10-12	fresh mushrooms, sliced	1/4	cup grated Parmesan cheese

Preheat oven to 350 degrees. Cook pasta according to package directions, using the minimum suggested cooking time, drain and set aside. In a large skillet, saute onion and mushrooms in butter until tender, about 3-5 minutes. In a large bowl, combine onion and mushrooms, chicken, pasta, spinach and cream. Season with salt and pepper and mix well. Pour mixture into a 2 quart casserole dish and sprinkle the top with a mixture of the bread crumbs and Parmesan cheese. Cover and bake for 30 minutes. Uncover and bake for 15 more minutes. Serve with grated Parmesan cheese on the side.

SERVES 2-3

*Depending on the kind of chicken you buy, poaching or boiling the chicken is the easiest way to cook it through. Place chicken in a pot with enough water to cover. Bring water to the simmering stage and simmer until tender, about 10 minutes. If you buy it with bones, boil the chicken first, then pull the meat off the bone in shreds.

CHICKEN, CHEESE AND BROCCOLI COMBO

15-20 minutes preparation and cooking time

An ideal meal to prepare when you come home late and want to eat in a hurry. It takes little time to prepare, yet boasts the flavor of hours of work.

  1   lb. whole boneless chicken breast, without skin
  1   tablespoon butter or margarine
  1   cup heavy cream
  1   tablespoon Dijon mustard
1/2   cup Cheddar or Swiss cheese, grated
  2   cups broccoli florets
  1   small tomato, chopped
1/2   teaspoon salt
1/4   teaspoon black pepper

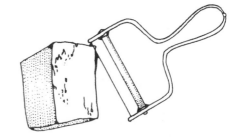

Blanche broccoli in a large pot of boiling water for 1 minute. Drain and set aside. Cut chicken into thin strips. In a large skillet, melt butter over medium heat. Add chicken and saute until golden brown. Stir in cream, mustard, and cheese and mix until cheese is melted and mixture is creamy. Stir in broccoli, tomato, salt and pepper. Mix well and serve over rice or pasta.

SERVES 2

COUNTRY STYLE CHICKEN PIE

20-25 minutes to prepare   12-15 minutes to bake

When you want a warm, hearty, country style meal in less than an hour, I suggest you try this recipe. This creamy chicken combination is topped with a sensational, bread-like, dough. Very filling!

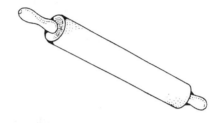

Filling:

1-2	tablespoons butter or margarine
1	small onion, chopped
2	tablespoons all-purpose flour
1	cup chicken broth
2	cups bite-size chicken pieces
1/2	cup frozen corn kernels

1/2	cup frozen sweet peas
6-8	fresh mushrooms, sliced
1/4	teaspoon black pepper
1/4	teaspoon dried thyme
1/4	teaspoon salt
1/4	cup sherry

Crust:

1	cup all-purpose flour
1	teaspoon baking powder
1/4	teaspoon salt

1	tablespoon butter
1/4	cup milk, possibly more
1	egg, lightly beaten

In a large sauce pan or skillet, saute onion in butter until tender. Add chicken and saute over medium high heat until chicken is golden brown. Sprinkle in flour and stir to coat chicken and onion. Gradually add chicken broth, and bring to a boil over medium-high heat, stirring constantly. Reduce heat to simmer and cook for 5 more minutes, or until mixture thickens to the consistency of gravy. Stir in corn, peas, mushrooms, pepper, thyme and salt. Heat through. Add sherry, mix well and pour mixture into a 2 quart casserole dish. Preheat oven to 450 degrees. To make the crust: Sift the flour, baking powder and salt into a large bowl or food processor fitted with the metal blade. Add butter and cut in with two knives or process until butter is pea size and mixture resembles coarse meal. Gradually add milk and stir with a fork, or process until a manageable dough forms (add more milk if mixture is too dry, a little at a time). Turn dough to a lightly floured surface and knead until smooth, 30-60 seconds. Roll dough out until it is large enough to cover the top of the casserole. Place on top of casserole (if chicken mixture does not come up to the top of the dish, push the dough down on top of the chicken and push up the sides to the rim). If desired, cut any excess dough that hangs over the rim of the dish and use to decorate the top. Brush the beaten egg on the surface of the dough, add any decorations, and brush again with egg. Prick the surface with a fork to allow steam to escape during baking. Bake for 12-15 minutes or until golden brown and bubbling out of steam vents. Cool slightly before serving.

SERVES 2-3

* 3

Beef

STEAK AND PEPPERS

1 hour preparation and cooking time

This dish is certain to become one of your favorites. The combination of steak and peppers served in a delicious sauce, is as tasty as it is easy.

1	lb. lean beef steak
1/4	cup soy sauce
1	clove garlic, whole
1/4	teaspoon ground ginger
1	tablespoon olive or vegetable oil
1	green pepper, sliced into thin strips
1	red pepper, sliced into thin strips
1	small onion, sliced
2	celery stalks, sliced
1	tablespoon cornstarch
1	cup water

Cut the steak, against the grain, into thin strips. Place in a small bowl with the soy sauce, ginger and garlic clove and set aside while you chop vegetables. Heat oil in a large skillet or wok and add meat mixture. Saute over high heat until brown on all sides, stirring constantly so the meat doesn't stick. Reduce heat and simmer for 30 minutes, until tender. Remove garlic clove, return to high heat and add vegetables. Saute until vegetables are tender crisp, about 7-10 minutes, stirring frequently. Mix cornstarch with water. Stir into beef mixture and simmer until sauce thickens, about 3-5 minutes, stirring constantly. Serve over rice or pasta.

SERVES 2-3

STEAK WITH SHELLS, BROCCOLI
AND FRESH HERBS

30-40 minutes preparation and cooking time

In this recipe, the steak is prepared separately and served with delightful blend of pasta, sour cream and fresh herbs. The combination is absolutely delicious.

1/2   lb. london broil*, trimmed of fat
  1   clove garlic, halved
1/2   8 oz. package medium pasta shells
  2   cups broccoli florets (or 1 head of fresh broccoli with the stalk cut away)
1/2   cup sour cream, more if necessary
1/4   cup fresh parsley, chopped
  2   tablespoons fresh basil, chopped
      Salt and ground black pepper for seasoning and to taste

Rub both sides of steak with garlic. Season with salt and pepper. Place 4" under broiler and broil for 5-6 minutes on each side for medium rare meat. Remove from oven and set aside. Cook pasta according to package directions. 1-2 minutes before pasta is done, add the broccoli to the pot. Cook until broccoli is tender-crisp, about 1 minute. Drain. Return the pasta and broccoli to the pan and add the sour cream, basil and parsley. Season with salt and pepper and mix well. (If mixture seems too dry, add more sour cream as necessary.) Slice the steak into thin strips. Spoon pasta mixture onto serving plate and arrange strips of steak along the side. Serve.

SERVES 2-3

*Ask your butcher or the meat counter at your grocer for smaller cuts of meat. If that's not possible, save leftover meat for sandwiches!

BELOVED BEEF POT PIE

45-55 minutes to prepare   *2 hours to bake (total)*

This meal is sure to warm your tummy on cold winter nights. Served with a roaring fire and a bottle of red wine, you'll forget all about the blizzard outside.

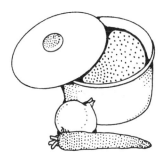

Filling:

1	tablespoon butter or margarine
1	lb. boneless beef chuck, cut into 1" cubes
1	medium onion, chopped
2	tablespoons all-purpose flour
1/2	teaspoon salt
1/4	teaspoon black pepper
1/4	teaspoon paprika

2   cups carrots, sliced diagonally into chunks   1/2   cup Sherry

2   stalks celery, sliced into chunks   1   tablespoon Dijon mustard

5   small new red potatoes, cut into eight pieces each

1   cup sweet corn (fresh or frozen)   1   teaspoon dried thyme

15   oz. can crushed tomatoes   1   egg

1   cup beef broth   1   tablespoon water

1   tablespoon dried parsley

Preheat oven to 350 degrees. In a large skillet, melt butter over medium high heat. Add beef and saute until brown on all sides. Remove from skillet and place in a large casserole dish. In the same skillet, saute the onion until tender, about 3-5 minutes. Add onion to beef. In a small bowl, combine flour, salt, pepper and paprika. Add flour mixture to beef and onion and stir until both are well coated. Add carrots, celery, potatoes, corn, crushed tomatoes, beef broth, Sherry, mustard, parsley and thyme. Mix well. Cover and bake for 1 hour. Uncover and bake for 30 more minutes. While you wait...

Pie Crust (top only):

1 1/2 cups all-purpose flour
  1/2 teaspoon salt
  1/2 cup (1 stick) butter, cold
  1/4 cup cold water

Sift the flour and salt into a large mixing bowl or into a food processor fitted with the metal blade. Cut the butter into small chunks and add to flour mixture. Cut butter into flour with two knives or process until butter is pea-size and mixture resembles coarse meal. Gradually add water and stir with a fork or process until a manageable dough forms. With the heal of your hand flatten dough out slightly, wrap in plastic wrap and refrigerate for at least 30 minutes.

In a small bowl, mix the egg and tablespoon of water. Remove stew from oven and pour into a clean 2 quart casserole dish. Roll out dough until it is 1" larger than the diameter of your casserole dish. Lay crust on top of casserole, leaving a 1" lip hanging over the edge. Brush the rim of the casserole dish with egg and pinch dough down around the edges. Brush the top of the pie with the egg and pierce the surface with a fork to allow steam to escape during cooking. Bake for 20-25 minutes, or until crust is golden and stew is bubbly out of steam vents.

SERVES 3-4

SLOPPY JOES

1 hour preparation and cooking time

This dish is guaranteed to be messy and will prove to be the best Sloppy Joe you've ever tasted. Served on warm Kaiser rolls, or homemade bread, these sandwiches will most certainly liven up your night or your lunchbox. In addition, this recipe is easy to double and even triple for company!

1	tablespoon butter or margarine		Pinch of cayenne pepper
1	small onion, chopped	1/4	teaspoon salt
1	stalk celery, chopped	1	teaspoon Worcestershire sauce
1	medium green pepper, chopped	3/4	cup ketchup
1	lb. ground beef	1/4	teaspoon dried basil
1/4	teaspoon chili powder	1/2	cup corn kernels
1/4	teaspoon black pepper	1 1/2	teaspoons Dijon mustard
		2	Italian plum tomatoes, chopped

Heat butter in a large skillet and add onion, celery and green pepper. Saute over medium heat until tender. Remove from skillet and set aside. Add meat to skillet and saute over medium heat, breaking up meat as is cooks, until completely browned. Add chili powder, black pepper, cayenne pepper and salt and mix well. Return vegetables to skillet and add remaining ingredients. Mix well, cover and simmer for 30-35 minutes, stirring frequently. If mixture seems dry, add more ketchup as necessary. Serve on warm rolls or bread.

SERVES 2-3

HOME-MADE CHEESE STEAK SANDWICHES

*25-30 minutes preparation
and cooking time*

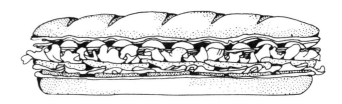

Sometimes you just feel the need for a cheese steak. It's a great, fun food to eat anytime. When you're tired of always going to the same take-out place for cheese steaks, try this home-made recipe. You may never eat take-out again!

1 lb. thinly sliced steak (or a smaller cut if you can get it)

Salt and black pepper	**2 tablespoons heavy cream**
2 tablespoons butter or margarine	**1/2 cup chopped tomatoes**
1 medium onion, sliced	**1 tablespoon Worcestershire sauce**
1 green bell pepper, sliced	**1 teaspoon Dijon mustard**
2 tablespoons all-purpose flour	**2 steak rolls, sliced in half horizontally and toasted**
3/4 cup beef broth	**1/2 cup Mozzarella or Cheddar cheese, grated**

Season both sides of the steak with salt and pepper. Heat 1 tablespoon of butter in a large skillet over medium high heat. Add steak and saute until brown on both sides. Remove from skillet and set aside. Add remaining butter to skillet and add onion and green pepper. Saute until tender and golden. Add flour to skillet and toss to coat vegetables evenly. Gradually add beef broth to pan, simmer over medium heat and deglaze the pan by scraping up the brown bits from the bottom and incorporating them into the broth. Once mixture has thickened, add cream, tomatoes, Worcestershire sauce and mustard. Reduce heat and simmer while you cut the steak into thin strips. Add the steak to the skillet and heat through. Sprinkle grated cheese on half of each roll and top with hot steak mixture. Serve warm.

SERVES 2

MEATBALLS WITH TWO VARIATION SAUCES

35-45 minutes preparation and cooking time

Looking for something different to enhance ordinary meatballs? Below are two suggestions. Depending on your mood, two different sauces are suggested, one creamy and one with a sweet and sour twist. The meatball recipe remains the same, just choose the sauce!

1 lb.	**lean ground beef**
2	**tablespoons chopped onion**
1/4	**cup bread crumbs**
2	**tablespoons fresh parsley, chopped**
1	**tablespoon butter or margarine**

In a large bowl, combine beef, onion, bread crumbs and parsley. Roll mixture into balls about 1 1/2" in size. In a large skillet, melt butter over medium-high heat until bubbly. Add meatballs and roll around in skillet until all sides are browned. Add one of two sauces as directed.

Variation I - Sweet and Sour Sauce

1	**can crushed pineapple**	1/2	**teaspoon black pepper**
2	**tablespoons brown sugar**	1	**tablespoon cornstarch**
1	**tablespoon soy sauce**	2	**tablespoons water**

Add pineapple, sugar, soy sauce and pepper to meatballs in skillet. Mix well, cover and simmer over medium low heat until meatballs are cooked through, about 10-12 minutes. Remove meatballs from skillet and set aside on serving platter. Dissolve cornstarch in water and stir into sauce. Stir until thickened, about 3-5 minutes. Pour sauce over meatballs and serve.

Variation II - Mushroom Cream Sauce

1	oz. dried shitake or porcini mushrooms	2	tablespoons all-purpose flour
2	cups beef broth	1/4	cup milk or light cream
1/8	cup dry red wine		Black pepper to taste

Soak dried mushrooms in 1/2 cup warm water for 20-30 minutes. Strain mushrooms through a colander lined with a paper towel, reserving juice. Pour reserved juice in with browned meatballs. Add beef broth and red wine. Rinse mushrooms under water to remove any grit, slice into small pieces and add to skillet. Simmer over medium low heat until meatballs are cooked through, about 10-12 minutes. Remove meatballs with a slotted spoon and set aside on serving platter. Dissolve flour in milk, stir into sauce and stir constantly with a wire whisk until mixture thickens. Pour sauce over meatballs and serve.

SERVES 2

MOM'S POT ROAST

20-30 minutes to prepare   *2 1/2 - 3 hours to cook*

This delicious combination of meat and vegetables provides a hearty meal for four. Allowed to simmer for several hours, the meat is tender and juicy, and boasts the flavor wine and spices.

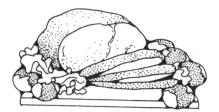

- 1 tablespoon olive or vegetable oil
- 1 3-4 lb. chuck roast, well trimmed
  Flour for dredging
- 1 small onion, chopped
- 2 cups beef broth
- 1 cup dry red wine
- 2 teaspoons dried thyme
- 1/2 teaspoon dried basil
- 1/2 teaspoon black pepper
- 6-8 small new red potatoes, quartered
- 5 carrots, sliced diagonally into large chunks
- 1 can or jar of pearl onions

Heat oil in a large stock pot over medium high heat. Dredge roast in flour and turn to coat all sides. Sear roast in hot oil, turning to brown all sides. When all sides are brown, add chopped onion, beef broth, red wine, thyme, basil and pepper. Bring to a boil, reduce heat and cover. Simmer for 2 1/2 - 3 hours, turning roast frequently to keep it moist. Add potatoes for the last 20-30 minutes of cooking. Roast is ready to serve when it easily falls apart when tested with a fork. Steam carrots in a small sauce pan until tender crisp. Just before serving, add carrots and pearl onions to pot roast and heat through. Place roast on serving platter and surround with vegetables. Remove surface grease from the simmering liquid and serve on the side with the roast and vegetables.

SERVES 4

TORNADOES OF BEEF

20-25 minutes preparation and cooking time

A delicious combination of steak and mushrooms. Perfect for entertaining when you have little preparation time.

1	lb. beef tenderloin, cut into bite size cubes
8-10	mushrooms, sliced
1-2	tablespoons butter or margarine
2	tablespoons Worcestershire sauce
1/4	teaspoon paprika
1	cup beef broth
2	tablespoons all-purpose flour
1/4	cup dry sherry
	Salt and black pepper to taste

In a large skillet, saute mushrooms in butter until tender and releasing juice. Remove mushrooms with a slotted spoon, reserving juice and set aside. Add beef to skillet and brown on all sides. Return mushrooms to skillet and stir in Worcestershire sauce and paprika. Stir in beef broth. Dissolve flour in sherry and add to skillet. Cook over medium heat until thickened, about 3-5 minutes, stirring constantly. Season with salt and black pepper and serve.

SERVES 2-4

STEAK WITH MUSHROOMS AND RED WINE

10-15 minutes preparation and cooking time

This is a basic recipe to enhance the flavor of steak. It's easy and it enables you to create a gourmet meal in minutes. Don't be afraid to add whatever spices you prefer to this recipe. When deciding what spice to add, try smelling what's cooking in the pot and then smelling the spice. If the two seem to mesh harmoniously, try it—in small quantities at first!

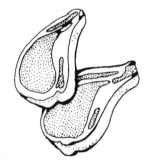

2	club steaks, about 1" thick
1	tablespoon butter or margarine
1	medium onion, chopped
8-10	fresh mushrooms, sliced
1/2	cup beef broth
1/2	cup dry red wine

The steak can be prepared several different ways, depending on your preference. Barbecue it on an outdoor grill for 5-7 minutes a side, place 4" under the broiler and broil for 3-5 minutes a side for medium rare meat or pan fry in a skillet with melted butter for about 3-5 minutes a side. (Times will vary depending on desired doneness). In a large skillet melt butter over medium heat. Add onion and mushrooms and saute until tender, about 3-5 minutes. Add beef broth, reduce heat and simmer until liquid is reduced by half. Add wine and cook until reduced by half again. Place steaks on serving plate, pour mushroom sauce over top and serve.

SERVES 2

MARINATED FLANK STEAK

5-10 minutes to prepare   *4 hours to marinate*   *8-12 minutes to cook*

If you've got the time to marinate, this is the perfect dish for meat lovers. Packed with flavor, this dish will become a favorite in your household.

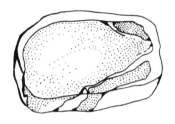

1	flank steak, 1 - 1 1/2 lbs.
	Black pepper
1/3	cup soy sauce
1/3	cup Sherry
2	tablespoons brown sugar
1/2	teaspoon dry mustard
1/4	teaspoon ground ginger

Season both sides of flank steak with pepper and place in a shallow baking dish. Combine all remaining ingredients, mix well and pour mixture over steak. Refrigerate for at least 4 hours, spooning marinade over the top once or twice if you can. Remove from pan and place 4" under broiler or on a barbecue grill. Broil for 4-6 minutes on each side for medium rare meat. Slice vertically and serve. Marinade may be strained, heated in a small sauce pan and served on the side, if desired.

SERVES 2-3

POCONO STEAK

20-30 minutes preparation and cooking time

I call this Pocono steak for the simple reason that I discovered it in the Poconos. I needed to prepare a hearty meal for a handful of people. I had the flank steak but needed to create a dish that would make the meat go further. By adding vegetables, there was plenty of food, the dish was a hit and it took just minutes to prepare!

1   lb. flank steak
2   tablespoons butter, margarine or oil
1   medium onion, chopped
1   can beef gravy
2   carrots, sliced julienne style
2   celery stalks, sliced julienne style
1   sweet red pepper, sliced
1   green bell pepper, sliced
1/2 cup dry red wine

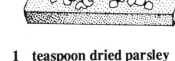

1   teaspoon dried parsley
1/2 teaspoon black pepper

You need to cut the steak into thin strips and this is the easiest way to do it: Cut the steak in half lengthwise, with the grain. Take one half and slice on an angle from the top down, going with the grain (if cut correctly, 2" squares will be the result). Stack squares on top of each other, using about 4-5 at a time, and slice into strips. Continue until all meat is sliced. In a large skillet, heat butter over high heat. Add onion and saute until tender. Stir in beef and quickly sear meat until brown on all sides. Remove meat and onion from pan and place in colander to drain off fat. Reduce heat to medium and add the gravy to the skillet. Stir in the wine, parsley and pepper. Add vegetables to pan and simmer until tender crisp, about 5-7 minutes. Return beef and onions to pan and heat through. Serve over pasta or rice.

SERVES 4-5

BEEF CASSEROLE WITH POTATOES AND CHEESE

20-25 minutes to prepare

50 minutes to bake

This casserole is simple to prepare and is perfect for evenings when you want something easy and tasty.

3-4	medium potatoes, unpeeled and sliced
1	lb. lean ground beef
1-2	tablespoons butter or margarine
1	small onion, chopped
1	red bell pepper, chopped into chunks
1	green bell pepper, chopped into chunks
1/4	teaspoon black pepper
2	tablespoons red wine vinegar
1	teaspoon dried parsley
1/4	teaspoon dried thyme
1/2	cup Swiss cheese, grated
1/2	teaspoon paprika

Preheat oven to 375 degrees. Melt butter in a large skillet over medium high heat. Add onion, red and green peppers and saute until tender, about 3-5 minutes. Add ground beef and saute over medium heat until cooked through, breaking up meat as it browns. If desired, drain beef mixture in collander, allowing fat to drip out, and return to pan. Stir in black pepper, vinegar, parsley and thyme. Spread meat mixture evenly into the bottom of a 2 quart casserole dish. Overlap potato slices to evenly cover beef mixture. Sprinkle grated Swiss cheese on top of potatoes, and sprinkle the paprika on top. Cover and bake 40 minutes. Uncover and bake for 10 minutes, or until potatoes are tender and cheese is golden brown. Serve.

SERVES 2-3

CHOP SUEY

20-25 minutes to prepare   *1 hour to bake*

This was, by far, my favorite dish as a child. My mother called it "Chop Suey", although I don't know where she got the name. A similar dish at a friend's house was called "S'MORE" for obvious reasons. Whatever you want to call it, you will certainly enjoy this dish, over and over again...

1 package elbow macaroni	1 can tomato soup
1 lb. ground beef	3-4 Italian plum tomatoes, chopped
1 tablespoon butter, margarine or oil	1/4 cup bread crumbs
2 celery stalks, chopped	1/4 cup Cheddar cheese, grated
1 medium onion, chopped	Salt and pepper to taste

Preheat oven to 350 degrees. Cook pasta according to package directions, using the minimum suggested cooking time, drain and set aside. In a large skillet, saute beef over medium heat until browned, breaking up meat as it cooks. Remove from skillet and drain in a colander, allowing fat to drip out. In the same skillet, melt the butter and add celery and onion. Saute over medium heat until tender. In a large bowl,

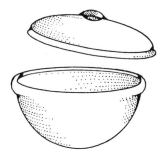

combine meat, celery, onion, tomato soup, tomatoes and cooked pasta. Season with salt and pepper. Pour mixture into a 2 quart casserole dish, sprinkle the top with a mixture of the bread crumbs and Cheddar cheese, cover and bake for 30 minutes. Uncover and bake for an additional 30 minutes. Serve with warm bread on the side if desired.

SERVES 2-3

4

Pork & Veal

BAKED HAM

10-15 minutes to prepare   *1 1/2 - 2 hours to bake*

Preparing a baked ham for guests is one of the easiest and
best tasting ways to impress your friends. You will be
amazed at how simple and delicious this recipe is.

1	**precooked, boneless ham, about 4-5 lbs.**
1/2	**cup honey**
2	**tablespoons Dijon mustard**
1	**packed tablespoon brown sugar**
20	**oz. can crushed pineapple**

Preheat oven to 325 degrees. If necessary, peel the skin
from ham, leaving a thin layer of fat. If ham is not already
scored, score fat with a sharp knife, by cutting diagonal
lines, criss-crossing to form diamond shapes on surface. Place the ham in a large shallow baking
pan lined with foil. In a small sauce pan, combine the honey, mustard and brown sugar. Simmer
over low heat until sugar is melted and mixture is smooth, stirring constantly. Brush honey
mixture over entire surface of ham and pour any remaining over top, allowing it to drip down the
sides. Pour crushed pineapple into bottom of baking dish. If you have one, insert a meat
thermometer into top of ham. Bake until internal temperature reaches 160-180 degrees, about 1
1/2 - 2 hours, basting frequently with the pan juices. Cool slightly before slicing and serve
warm or cold.

SERVES 4-6 (leftovers make great ham sandwiches!)

BARBECUED SPARE RIBS

20-30 minutes to prepare   *4 hours to marinate*   *40-50 minutes to bake*

This recipe of my mothers is the best tasting rib recipe ever. A bit time consuming, but worth it!

1	**rack spare ribs, about 2 lbs.**
1-2	**tablespoons butter or margarine**
1	**small onion, chopped**
2	**cloves garlic, crushed**
1	**18 oz. bottle of your favorite barbecue sauce**
12	**oz. flat dark beer**
1	**tablespoon German or Dijon mustard**
1	**tablespoon Worcestershire sauce**
1	**tablespoon lemon juice**
1	**packed tablespoon dark brown sugar**
1	**tablespoon red wine vinegar**

Parboil ribs by immersing them into rapidly boiling water for 2 minutes. If the ribs are split, parboil them in shifts so as not to disturb the boiling. Set ribs aside. Heat butter in a large sauce pan over medium heat. Add onion and garlic and saute until tender, about 3-5 minutes. Stir in remaining ingredients and bring to a boil. Reduce heat and simmer for 10 minutes. Place ribs in a large shallow dish and cover with barbecue sauce. Marinate at room temperature or refrigerate at least 4 hours. Preheat outdoor grill. Barbecue ribs on the grill until tender on the inside and crisp on the outside, about 40-45 minutes, basting frequently with sauce.   If you do not plan to use an outdoor grill, preheat oven to 450 degrees. Place ribs in a roasting pan and bake until tender, about 50 minutes, basting frequently with the sauce.

SERVES 2

PORK CHOPS IN LEMON SAUCE

15-20 minutes preparation and cooking time

This tangy pork dish is deliciously light and takes little time to prepare. When you are tired of the ordinary, try this little number...you'll be sweetly surprised.

2	**pork loin butterfly chops, 3/4" thick**
1	**tablespoon butter or margarine**
1/4	**cup scallions, chopped**
1	**teaspoon grated fresh lemon peel**
1/2	**cup fresh lemon juice**
1	**tablespoon honey**
1	**tablespoon soy sauce**
1/4	**teaspoon dried ginger**
1	**tablespoon cornstarch**
1/2	**cup water**

In a large skillet, saute scallions and lemon peel in butter until tender, about 2-3 minutes. Remove from pan and set aside. In the same skillet (add more butter if necessary) saute pork chops over medium heat until golden brown on both sides. Return scallions and lemon to pan and add lemon juice, honey, soy sauce and ginger. Cover and simmer until pork is cooked through, about 10 minutes. Remove pork chops from pan and place on serving plate. Dissolve cornstarch in water and add to pan. Simmer over medium heat until sauce thickens, about 3-5 minutes, stirring constantly. Pour sauce over pork chops and serve.

SERVES 2

PORK CHOP CASSEROLE

15-20 minutes to prepare   *30-35 minutes to bake*

The name of this dish may sound a bit odd, however the result is a very flavorful, unique dish.

2-3	boneless pork chops	1	cup milk
1-2	tablespoons butter or margarine	2	tablespoons all-purpose flour
8 oz.	package egg noodles	1/2	cup sour cream
1	small onion, chopped	1	teaspoon oregano
1	medium green pepper, chopped	1/4	teaspoon black pepper
3	stalks celery, minced		

Preheat oven to 350 degrees. Cook egg noodles according to package directions, using the minimum suggested cooking time. Drain and set aside (if the noodles are finished before you are ready to blend ingredients, stir in some milk to keep noodles from sticking). In a large skillet, sear the pork chops in hot butter over high heat until golden brown on both sides. Remove chops and set aside. Reduce heat and add onion, green pepper and celery to the skillet. Saute until tender, about 3-5 minutes. Dissolve flour in milk and stir into vegetables. Simmer, stirring constantly until mixture thickens, about 3-5 minutes. Stir in sour cream, oregano and pepper. Combine egg noodles and milk mixture in a 2 quart casserole dish. Lay pork chops on top of noodles and press down slightly. Cover and bake for 30-35 minutes, or until pork is cooked through. Serve.

SERVES 2-3

HINT: For great leftovers: add tomato sauce or tomato soup to pasta mixture, mix well and reheat.

STUFFED PORK CHOPS

20-25 minutes to prepare   *1 hour and 15 minutes to bake*

The stuffing in this recipe is a combination of bread, apples, raisins and yogurt. The mixture may sound unusual, but the result is a tender, juicy chop filled with a sweet, flavorful stuffing.

2	pork chops, with or without the bone	1	cup plain yogurt
1	tablespoon butter or margarine	1	tablespoon oregano
	Flour for dredging	1/2	teaspoon salt
2	cups unseasoned bread cubes (or day old white bread cut into cubes)		
2	celery stalks, chopped	1/2	teaspoon black pepper
1	cup chopped apples	1/2	cup water or white wine
1/2	cup raisins		

Preheat oven to 350 degrees. In a large bowl, combine the bread cubes, celery, apple, raisins, yogurt, oregano, salt and pepper and mix well. Set aside. If you have chops on the bone, cut meat away from bone. Melt butter over medium-high heat in a large skillet. Dredge chops in flour and turn to coat both sides. Sear chops in butter by placing in hot skillet and quickly browning both sides. Remove from skillet and cut a large gash or pocket in one side of each chop. Stuff bread mixture loosely into opening in chops until overflowing with stuffing. Place in shallow baking dish and set aside. Deglaze the skillet by adding 1/2 cup water or wine, bring to simmering stage and scrape up the brown bits from the bottom of the pan (incorporating them into the sauce). Simmer over medium heat until liquid is reduced by half. Pour sauce over chops, cover with foil and bake for 1 hour and 15 minutes. Extra stuffing may be placed in a covered casserole dish and baked along with the pork chops for the last 45 minutes. Remove the lid from the stuffing for the last 15 minutes of cooking, to brown the surface. Serve extra stuffing on the side.

SERVES 2

VEAL WITH MUSHROOMS AND WHITE WINE

30 minutes preparation and cooking time

A savory, gourmet meal in minutes.

> 1 **lb. veal (use trimmed top, bottom round or debone a veal chop)**
> 2 **tablespoons butter or margarine**
> 1 **shallot, chopped**
> 8-10 **fresh mushrooms, sliced**
> 1/3 **cup all-purpose flour**
> 1/2 **teaspoon paprika**
>   **Juice of 1 whole lemon**
> 1/2 **cup white wine**

Salt and pepper to taste

Trim excess fat from veal. Place between two pieces of plastic wrap and pound until about 1/4" thick (if you don't have a meat tenderizer, use a rubber hammer or press firmly with a rolling pin). Set veal aside. In a large skillet melt 1 tablespoon of the butter over medium-high heat. Add shallot and saute until tender, about 3-5 minutes. Add mushrooms and saute until tender and releasing juice. Remove shallot and mushrooms from skillet and set aside. Combine flour and paprika in a small bowl. Dredge veal in flour mixture and coat well. Melt remaining tablespoon of butter in skillet and add veal. Saute over medium heat until golden brown on both sides. Add lemon juice and wine and bring mixture to a boil. Reduce heat to simmer, return shallot and mushrooms to pan, cover and simmer for 20 minutes. While veal simmers, stir occasionally and incorporate the brown bits from the bottom of the pan. Season with salt and pepper and serve.

SERVES 2

BAKED VEAL WITH RICE

20-25 minutes to prepare   *50-60 minutes to bake*

This is a unique and exquisite way to prepare veal. You assemble the casserole and the oven does the rest. It's easy and delicious.

3/4	lb. veal, cut into bite size chunks
1	tablespoon butter or margarine
8-10	fresh mushrooms, sliced
1	cup uncooked white, brown or wild rice
1	small onion, chopped
1	small green bell pepper, chopped
1/2	teaspoon paprika
1/4	teaspoon salt
1/4	teaspoon black pepper
2 1/4	cups beef broth

Preheat oven to 350 degrees. In a large skillet, heat butter over medium high heat. Add veal and saute until brown on all sides. Add mushrooms to skillet and saute until tender and releasing juice. In a two quart casserole dish combine uncooked rice, onion and green pepper. Add paprika, salt and pepper and mix well. Stir in veal and mushrooms. Add beef broth and mix well. Cover and bake for 50-60 minutes or until liquid is absorbed and rice is fluffy, stirring occasionally. Serve.

SERVES 2

Seafood

FLOUNDER FLORENTINE

5-10 minutes to prepare   *10-12 minutes to bake*

My friend Karyn discovered this dish strictly because of the ingredients in her refrigerator—thank goodness. I recommend this dish when you want a deliciously light gourmet meal in less than 20 minutes.

- 2 flounder fillets (approximately 8 oz. each)
  Salt and black pepper to taste
- 1 lemon
- 1 clove garlic, minced
- 1 package frozen spinach, cooked and drained
- 1/2 lb. Swiss cheese, grated

Preheat oven to 375 degrees. Place flounder fillets on a baking sheet and season with salt and pepper. Squeeze lemon juice over each fillet. Spread garlic evenly over each fillet. Cover fillets evenly with cooked spinach. Top with grated Swiss cheese and bake for 10-12 minutes, or until fish pulls apart easily when tested with a fork. Serve immediately.

SERVES 2

FLOUNDER IN WHITE WINE

5-10 minutes to prepare
30 minutes to bake

This refreshing fish dish is prepared
with vegetables. The wine and
vegetables enhance the fresh taste of
flounder and create and colorful dish
that is appealing to the eye as well as
the palate.

- 2   **fresh flounder fillets,
      about 8 oz. each**
- 1   **medium onion, sliced**
- 1   **package frozen asparagus, thawed and drained**
- 2   **carrots, peeled and cut julienne style**
- 1/2 **cup dry white wine**
- 2   **tablespoons fresh lemon juice
      Salt and black pepper to taste**

Preheat oven to 350 degrees. Blanche asparagus and carrots in a large pot of boiling water for 2
minutes. Drain, rinse under cold water to prevent further cooking and set aside. Spread half of
the sliced onion in the bottom of a shallow baking dish. Place fillets on top, season with salt and
pepper and cover with remaining onion. Alternate asparagus and carrot slices on top of fillets.
Pour wine and lemon juice over top. Bake for 30 minutes, or until fish pulls apart when tested
with a fork. I suggest basting the fish 1 or 2 times during cooking by spooning the wine and
juice over the vegetables on top—it will prevent everything from drying out. Serve
immediately.

SERVES 2

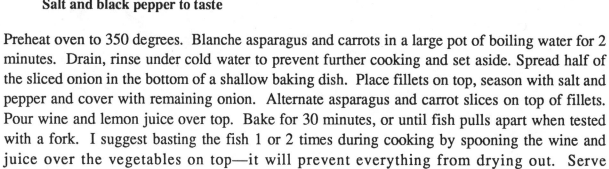

FLOUNDER PARMESAN

40-45 minutes preparation and cooking time

This unique way to prepare flounder tastes sensational. It's a nice change from the usual lemon or wine recipes.

 2 flounder fillets, about 8 oz. each
    Salt and black pepper
    All-purpose flour
 1 egg, slightly beaten
1/4 cup seasoned bread crumbs
1/4 cup grated Parmesan cheese
1/4 teaspoon paprika
1-2 tablespoons butter or margarine

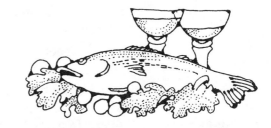

Sauce:

2	tablespoons chopped onion	1/2	teaspoon salt
15	oz. tomato sauce	1/4	teaspoon black pepper
1/2	teaspoon granulated sugar	1/4	teaspoon thyme

Season flounder on both sides with salt and pepper. Dust with flour on both sides. In a shallow dish, combine the bread crumbs, Parmesan cheese and paprika. Dip fish into the eggs and then into bread crumb mixture. Set aside or refrigerate while you prepare the sauce. Combine all sauce ingredients in a small sauce pan. Simmer over low heat for 15 minutes. Heat butter in a large skillet until bubbly. Add flounder and saute over medium heat until both sides are golden and fish pulls apart when tested with a fork, about 15 minutes. Place fish on serving platter and spoon tomato sauce on top. Serve warm.

SERVES 2

TOM'S GRILLED SWORDFISH

5 minutes to prepare   *12-15 minutes to cook*

Using Tom's famous barbecue sauce, this swordfish is packed with flavor, and enables you to prepare a fabulous meal in minutes.

1	swordfish steak, about 1 lb.
1/2	cup white wine vinegar
1/4	cup vegetable oil
1	egg
1	teaspoon salt
1/2	teaspoon black pepper
1/4	teaspoon paprika

Preheat outdoor grill or broiler. In a small bowl, combine all ingredients but the swordfish and mix well with a wire whisk. Brush a generous amount of sauce on both sides of swordfish steak. Broil about 4" from heat source, turning over and basting every 3 minutes. Fish is cooked through when it can be pulled apart when tested with a fork. Serve hot.

SERVES 2

BAKED RED SNAPPER WITH FRESH TOMATOES

20-25 minutes to prepare   *15 minutes to bake*

This recipe is a simple and refreshing way to prepare snapper. If desired, serve with rice seasoned with saffron or a mixture of fresh vegetables for a colorful plate. A perfect dish for entertaining.

1   large red snapper fillet, about 1/2 lb.
4   medium ripe tomatoes
1   tablespoon butter or margarine
1/2 cup dry white wine
2   tablespoons fresh lemon juice
1/2 teaspoon salt
1/2 teaspoon dried thyme
1/2 teaspoon dried parsley
1/4 teaspoon paprika

Skin tomatoes: slice an X on the bottom of each tomato, stab the stem end with a fork and immerse into rapidly boiling water for 10 seconds. Remove from water and peel skin off with ease. Preheat oven to 425 degrees. Slice each tomato into 8 wedges and remove seeds with a small spoon. Melt butter in a large skillet over medium heat. Add tomatoes and saute until tender, about 3-5 minutes. Stir in wine, lemon juice, salt, thyme, parsley and paprika. Simmer until heated through. Pour mixture into shallow baking dish and place snapper fillet, skin side down on top. Spoon some tomato/wine sauce on top of fillet. Bake for 15 minutes or until fish pulls apart when tested with a fork. Serve snapper with tomato sauce on top or on the side.

SERVES 2

FILLET OF SOLE WITH ORANGE

15 minutes to prepare   *20 minutes to bake*

A different approach to preparing sole. The orange adds a refreshing taste to this delicate flavored fish.

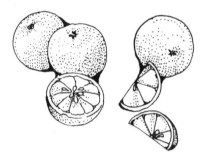

1	lb. fillet of sole
	Salt and white pepper
1	orange
1/2	cup dry vermouth
8-10	fresh mushrooms, sliced
1	tablespoon butter or margarine
1/2	teaspoon dried thyme
2	tablespoons minced onion

Preheat oven to 350 degrees. Season both sides of fillet with salt and white pepper, place in a lightly greased, shallow baking dish and set aside. Cut orange in half. Squeeze the juice from one half into a small bowl and slice the other half into 1/4" thick slices. Add vermouth to orange juice and pour mixture over fillet. Saute mushrooms in butter until tender. Sprinkle the surface of the fillet with thyme. Top with an even layer of minced onion followed by sauteed mushrooms.   Arrange orange slices in a row on top of mushrooms. Bake for 20 minutes or until fish pulls apart when tested with a fork. Remove orange slices from surface before serving and serve as garnish.

SERVES 2

BAKED SALMON WITH HORSERADISH MAYONNAISE

5-10 minutes to prepare *12-14 minutes to bake*

Another dish perfect for entertaining (increase ingredients accordingly).

2	fresh salmon fillets
	Salt and black pepper
1	whole lemon
1/2	cup mayonnaise (or 1/4 cup mayonaisse and 1/4 cup plain yogurt)
1	tablespoon Dijon mustard
1	tablespoon horseradish
1	teaspoon dill weed

Preheat oven to 400 degrees. Place salmon fillets in a shallow baking dish and season the top with salt and pepper. Slice lemon in half and squeeze the juice from one half over fillets. Slice the remaining half to use as garnish. Bake salmon for 12-14 minutes, or until fish pulls apart when tested with a fork. In a small sauce pan, combine mayonnaise, mustard, horseradish and dill. Heat over low heat until just heated through. Serve fillets with lemon slices and mayonnaise mixture on the side.

SERVES 2

SHRIMP STIR-FRY

20-25 minutes preparation and cooking time

This recipe is a deliciously light way to prepare shrimp. Using a wok or heavy skillet enables you to create this fabulous meal in minutes.

1	lb. large shrimp, cooked or uncooked
1-2	tablespoons sesame, peanut or vegetable oil
1	medium onion, chopped
1	clove garlic, minced
2	stalks celery, chopped
1	red bell pepper, sliced
1/2	lb. snow peas, ends trimmed
1	teaspoon grated fresh ginger, or 1/2 teaspoon dried
1/4	cup soy sauce
1/4	cup water
2	teaspoons red wine vinegar
1	tablespoon cornstarch

If the shrimp is uncooked, simmer it in enough water to cover until tender, about 10-12 minutes. Drain, peel and remove vein along the back of each shrimp. Slice in half and set aside. Heat oil in wok or large skillet and add onion and garlic. Saute over medium-high heat until tender, about 3-5 minutes, stirring frequently. Add celery, red pepper and snow peas and saute until tender crisp, about 3-4 minutes. Stir in shrimp and ginger and heat through. In a small bowl, combine the soy sauce, water, vinegar and cornstarch. Stir into shrimp mixture, and simmer until sauce thickens, stirring constantly. Serve over rice.

SERVES 2

LEMON SHRIMP

20-25 minutes preparation and cooking time

When you're looking for a light, refreshing meal, try this easy recipe for shrimp. Depending on how quickly you peel the shrimp, the preparation time can be just minutes, and the result is divine.

1 - 1 1/2	lbs. large shrimp, uncooked
1/3	cup all-purpose flour
1/4	cup grated Parmesan cheese
1/2	teaspoon salt
1/4	teaspoon ground black pepper
1/4	teaspoon cayenne pepper
1/4	teaspoon dry mustard
2	eggs, slightly beaten
2	tablespoons butter or margarine
	Juice of 1 lemon, about 1/4 cup
1/8	cup Sherry

Peel shrimp, leaving tail on, and devein by removing the dark vein just underneath the surface. In a small bowl, combine flour, cheese, salt, black pepper, cayenne pepper and mustard. Dip shrimp into eggs and then dredge in flour mixture, coating well. In a large skillet, melt butter over medium heat. Add a portion of the shrimp and saute for 2 minutes on each side, until golden. Remove from skillet and keep warm. Continue until all shrimp are cooked. Stir lemon juice and Sherry into remaining butter and brown bits in the pan. Simmer gently, stirring constantly to incorporate the brown bits into the liquid. Pour sauce over shrimp and serve.

SERVES 2

KARYN'S SHRIMP SCAMPI

15-20 minutes to prepare   *5-10 minutes to cook*

For garlic lovers, this dish is a must!

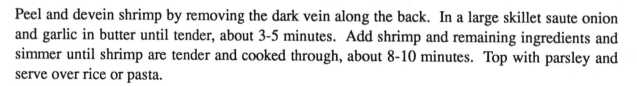

-   2   **lbs. medium shrimp, uncooked**
-   1/4 **cup chopped green onion**
-   4   **cloves garlic, minced**
-   3/4 **cup butter**
-   1/4 **cup dry white wine**
-   2   **tablespoons fresh lemon juice**
-   1/2 **teaspoon salt**
-   1/4 **teaspoon black pepper**
-   1   **tablespoon fresh parsley, chopped**

Peel and devein shrimp by removing the dark vein along the back. In a large skillet saute onion and garlic in butter until tender, about 3-5 minutes. Add shrimp and remaining ingredients and simmer until shrimp are tender and cooked through, about 8-10 minutes. Top with parsley and serve over rice or pasta.

SERVES 2-4

KARYN'S MUSSELS MARINARA

10-15 minutes to prepare   *1-2 hours to cook*

The following dish is prepared using mussels, but it can be made with any and all types of seafood. The sauce can be used to simmer your favorite fish, for steaming shrimp, scallops or clams, or used to stew a combination of seafood to create a medley of wonderful flavors.

1 1/2 - 2 lbs. fresh mussels	1 teaspoon dried parsley
28 oz. can crushed tomatoes	1/2 teaspoon dried basil
6 oz. can tomato paste	1/2 teaspoon rosemary
2 cloves garlic, minced	1/2 cup dry red wine
1 bay leaf	1 cup water
1/2 teaspoon salt	1/2 lb. spaghetti or linguine
1/4 teaspoon black pepper	
1/2 teaspoon crushed red pepper	

Scrub mussel shells thoroughly and remove beards (the beard is the coarse material sticking out of the shell - it can be snipped off with a pair of scissors). Refrigerate mussels until ready to use. Combine remaining ingredients (except mussels) in a large stock pot or sauce pan and bring to a boil. Reduce heat and simmer 1-2 hours, stirring occasionally. When close to serving time, cook pasta according to package directions, drain and set aside. Just before serving, add mussels to the pot and simmer until mussels open, about 5-7 minutes. Discard bay leaf and any shells that do not open. Serve mussels and sauce over pasta.

SERVES 2

6

Soup

CORN AND POTATO CHOWDER

1 hour preparation and cooking time

For those nights when you just don't feel like a big dinner, when soup and a sandwich will do, try this wonderful, hearty chowder that's almost as easy to prepare as opening a can of Campbell's.

1	tablespoon butter or margarine
1	small onion, chopped
2	celery stalks, chopped
4	cups fresh or frozen sweet corn
4	medium new red potatoes, peeled and chopped into small chunks
1/2	teaspoon salt
1/4	teaspoon black pepper
1/2	teaspoon thyme
1/2	teaspoon dried basil
1	teaspoon dried parsley
1	cup water
1	cup milk, more as needed

In a large sauce pan, saute the onion in butter over medium heat until tender, about 3-5 minutes. Add celery and cook for 5 more minutes. Add corn, salt, pepper, thyme, basil and parsley. Mix well, cover and cook for 5 minutes, allowing all the spices to combine. Add water and simmer for 10-15 minutes. Remove 1 cup of chowder from pan and puree in a food processor fitted with the metal blade or a blender. Return puree to pan and add potatoes and milk. Simmer until potatoes are tender, about 30-35 minutes, stirring frequently and adding more milk if necessary. Serve.

SERVES 2-3

KARYN'S BEAN SOUP

5 minutes - day ahead preparation   *preparation day - 2 hours to cook*

This rich, hearty soup almost has the consistency of chili. The longer the soup is allowed to simmer, the more dramatic and wonderful the flavor.

16	oz. package mixed dried beans
1	medium yellow onion, chopped
2	cans condensed beef broth
2	quarts water
3-4	carrots, sliced into chunks
1/2	cup barley

Rinse beans in water, discard any foriegn materials (stones, etc.) and soak in enough water to cover overnight (at least 24 hours). Drain beans and pour into a large sauce pan or stock pot. Add all remaining ingredients and bring to a boil over high heat. Reduce heat and simmer for at least 2 hours. Serve hot.

SERVES 2-4

RED ONION SOUP

1 1/2 hours preparation and cooking time

The aroma of this soup cooking is one of the best! The sweet smell of red onions simmering with red wine will fill your home with an enticing aroma that begs to be tasted before dinner-time. This variation of traditional onion soup is so tasty that you may never go back to the original. It's a hearty, delicious soup that is good enough to be served as a meal - it's very filling!

- **5 large red onions**
- **2 tablespoons butter or margarine**
- **1 cup dry red wine**
- **4 cups beef broth**
- **1/2 teaspoon dried thyme**
- **2 tablespoons fresh parsley, chopped (optional)**
- **French roll**
- **1/2 cup Swiss cheese, grated**
- **Salt and freshly ground black pepper to taste**

Cut onions into quarters and slice into 1/4" thick slices. Melt butter in a large stock pot and add onions. Simmer over low heat until onions are tender, about 35-40 minutes. Add red wine and simmer for 10 minutes. Add beef broth and thyme and simmer for 15 minutes. Preheat oven to 400 degrees. Slice French roll into 1" slices and place 4 of the slices on a baking sheet. Bake until golden brown, about 10 minutes. Remove from oven and divide cheese evenly on top of bread. Season the top of each slice with salt and pepper. Return to oven and bake until cheese is melted and golden, about 5-10 minutes. Place bread in soup bowls. Stir parsley into onion soup and ladle hot soup over bread in bowls. Serve hot.

SERVES 2-4

DAWN'S VEGETABLE SOUP

10-15 minutes to prepare   *1 hour to cook*

This simple and heavenly recipe for vegetable soup combines a unique variety of fresh garden vegetables. It takes just minutes to prepare and allows you some free time before you eat. Also, the perfect soup to prepare in advance and freeze until ready to use. After defrosting, reheat soup in a large stock pot or sauce pan before serving.

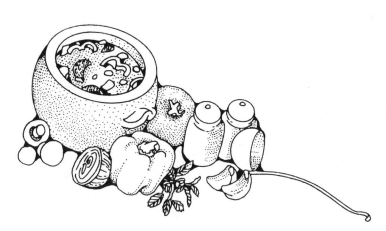

1	tablespoon vegetable oil
1/2	head cabbage, chopped
4	carrots, chopped into chunks
2	celery stalks, chopped
1	medium zucchini, chopped
1/2	lb. fresh mushrooms, sliced
2	cans beef broth (totaling about 4 cups of liquid)
28	oz. can crushed tomatoes
1/2	teaspoon ground black pepper

Heat oil in a large stock pot or sauce pan and add vegetables. Saute over medium heat until tender, about 5-7 minutes. Add remaining ingredients and bring to a boil. Reduce heat, cover and simmer for 1 hour. Cool slightly before serving.

SERVES 3-4

HINT: For a heartier soup, add pasta or rice!

CHICKEN SOUP WITH DUMPLINGS

10-15 minutes to prepare   *1 hour and 15 minutes to cook*

Everyone's mother makes the BEST chicken soup. It doesn't matter how sick you are, her soup always makes you feel better. Well, I dare you to try this recipe. It's simple, yet fabulously delicious. I promise I won't tell... In addition, dumplings are added to this chicken soup to create a rich, hearty meal.

1	3 lb. chicken cut into 8 pieces (you can buy it pre-cut)
3	quarts water
4	chicken bouillon cubes (optional)
1	large yellow onion, chopped
3-4	large carrots, unpeeled and cut into large chunks
3-4	whole celery stalks, cut into large pieces
1	bay leaf
1	teaspoon dried thyme
10	black peppercorns
1/2	teaspoon sage
1/4	cup fresh parsley, chopped
8	oz. package egg noodles

Dumplings:

1   cup plus 2 tablespoons all-purpose flour
1/4   teaspoon baking soda
1   teaspoon baking powder
     Pinch salt
2   tablespoons butter
1/2   cup buttermilk
1/4   cup fresh parsley

Place chicken pieces in a large stock pot and cover with water. Add all remaining ingredients except parsley, noodles and dumplings. Bring to a boil over high heat. Reduce heat and simmer for 1 hour. To prepare the dumplings (try to prepare the dumplings as close to eating time as possible): In a large bowl or food processor fitted with the metal blade, combine flour, baking soda, baking powder, salt and butter. Cut in with two knives or process until mixture resembles coarse meal. Gradually add buttermilk and parsley and blend or process until combined. Set aside until ready to use. Remove chicken stock from heat and drain the broth into a large pot or bowl. (At this point you may discard the vegetables; I keep the carrots in my soup.) Skim the fat from the broth. Peel skin off chicken pieces and pull meat off the bone, allowing the meat to come off in shreds. Discard skin and bones. Bring soup stock back to a boil and add noodles. Reduce heat to simmer and drop in 6 tablespoons of the dumpling mixture on top of broth, allowing space between dumplings. Cover with a lid and cook for 5 minutes. Turn dumplings over, return lid and cook for 5 more minutes. Place dumplings on serving plate, stir chicken and parsley into noodles and serve in bowls alongside dumplings.

SERVES 3-4

7

Bread

HALF WHITE - HALF WHOLE WHEAT BREAD

20-25 minutes to prepare   *1 hour and 45 minutes to rise*
55 minutes to bake

The perfect bread for anytime! Delicious served warm with dinner, used in sandwich making, or just plain by itself.

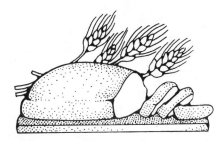

1 packet dry active yeast	1/4 packed cup light brown sugar
1 cup milk	1 3/4 cups all-purpose white flour
1/4 cup vegetable oil	1 3/4 cups whole wheat flour
1 egg	

Warm the milk to lukewarm over low heat or in the microwave (if you use the microwave, allow a few minutes before adding yeast). Sprinkle yeast over milk and set aside to dissolve. In a small bowl, combine the oil, egg and sugar and mix well with a wire whisk. Add milk mixture and mix well. In a large bowl, combine the two flours and make a well in the center. Pour the milk mixture into the center of the well and mix ingredients together with a fork. Turn to a lightly floured surface and knead for 10 minutes, continually re-flouring the surface if the dough sticks. Place dough in a lightly oiled bowl and turn to coat all sides. Cover with a dish towel and let rise in a warm place, free from draft, until doubled in bulk, about 1 hour. Punch your fist into middle of dough, remove from bowl and knead briefly. Place in a lightly greased bread pan, cover and let rise in a warm place until doubled in bulk, about 45 minutes.

Preheat oven to 375 degrees. Bake loaf for 15 minutes, reduce heat to 325 degrees and bake for and additional 40 minutes.

For a soft crust, brush the top of loaf with melted butter while still warm.

VARIATION: Use honey instead of brown sugar for different sweet taste.

FRENCH BREAD

20 minutes to prepare   *2 hours to rise*
30 minutes to bake

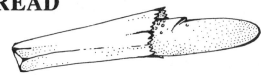

Next time you invite guests over for dinner, amaze
them with homemade french bread (just don't tell how easy it was to make). This bread is an
ideal companion for almost all pasta dishes and tastes fabulous with chili!

1	**packet dry active yeast**	1/2	**tablespoon butter or margarine, melted**
1 1/4	**cups lukewarm water**	3 1/2	**cups all-purpose flour**
1 1/2	**teaspoons salt**	1	**egg white, slightly beaten**
			mixed with 1 tablespoon cold water

In a large bowl, dissolve yeast in warm water.   Add salt, butter and flour and mix with a fork
until flour is absorbed. If you have a mixer fitted with a dough hook, mix for 2 minutes and then
process on the kneading speed for 2-4 minutes. If you do not have a dough hook, turn to a lightly
floured surface and knead for 8-10 minutes, or until smooth and elastic. Place in a lightly oiled
bowl and turn to coat all sides. Cover with a dish towel and let rise in a warm place, free from
draft until doubled in bulk, about 1 hour. Punch dough down with your fist and remove from
bowl. Roll dough out with a rolling pin or the heel of your hands to form a 12 X 15 inch oblong.
Roll up tightly from the longer side, tapering the ends as you go. Place on lightly greased baking
sheet, cover with dish towel and let rise in a warm place until doubled in bulk, about 45 minutes.

Preheat oven to 450 degrees. Make 3-4 diagonal slices, about 1/4" deep, on the top of the loaf.
Bake at 450 degrees for 25 minutes. Remove from oven, decrease oven temperature to 425
degrees, and brush the bread with the egg white and water mixture. Return to oven and bake for
5 minutes. Cool on rack before serving.

MAKES 1 LOAF

OAT-BUTTERMILK BREAD

15-20 minutes to prepare   *50-55 minutes to bake*

Prepare this bread when you're looking for an all-purpose bread. It's fabulous with butter or preserves, makes for delicious hearty sandwiches, and is perfect at dinner-time to soak up precious juices. In addition, see the variation that follows the directions for a different flavored bread.

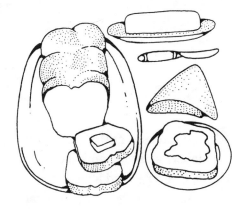

2 1/2 **cups all-purpose flour**
   2 **teaspoons baking powder**
   1 **teaspoon baking soda**
1/2 **teaspoon salt**   2 **egg whites**
3/4 **cup rolled oats, not instant**   2 **cups buttermilk**
                                                2 **tablespoons butter or margarine, melted**

Preheat oven to 350 degrees. Sift together the flour, baking powder, baking soda and salt into a large bowl. Stir in oats with a fork. Make a well in the center and set aside. In a separate bowl, combine the egg whites, buttermilk and melted butter. Mix well with a wire whisk. Pour mixture into the center of flour mixture. Fold in with a spatula until just combined, do not overmix. Pour batter into a lightly greased bread pan and bake for 50-55 minutes, or until a knife comes out clean. Cool in pan on rack 10 minutes before removing from pan. Tastes best when served warm.

MAKES 1 LOAF

Variation: For a sweeter bread, take out 1/2 cup buttermilk and replace it with maple syrup or honey. This sweet bread may also be enhanced with 1/2 tsp. cinnamon or 1/2 tsp. lemon rind.

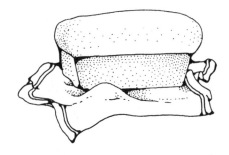

AMAZING APPLE BREAD

25-30 minutes to prepare   *1 hour to bake*

This refreshing bread is a nice change from the usual banana bread, is simple to prepare and provides a perfect use for that bushel of fall apples sitting in your kitchen. Also makes a nice gift during the holiday season.

2 1/2	packed cups grated tart apple (i.e., Mackintosh - leave the skin on for extra flavor)*		
2	tablespoons lemon juice	1	egg
1/2	teaspoon grated lemon rind	2	cups all-purpose flour
1/4	packed cup light brown sugar	2	teaspoons baking powder
1/4	cup honey	1/2	teaspoon baking soda
2	tablespoons butter or margarine, melted	1/4	teaspoon salt
2	tablespoons milk	1 1/4	teaspoons cinnamon

Preheat oven to 350 degrees. In a small bowl, combine grated apple, lemon juice and lemon rind. Mix well and set aside. In a large bowl, combine brown sugar, honey, butter, milk and egg and mix well with a wire whisk. Stir in apple mixture and mix well. Sift together the dry ingredients into a large bowl and make a well in the center. Pour the apple mixture into the center and fold together with a wooden spoon or spatula until completely combined. Pour batter into lightly greased bread pan and bake for 1 hour, or until a knife comes out clean. Cool on rack before removing from pan.

MAKES 1 LOAF

* I like to leave some apple chunks slightly larger to create a hearty bread where you can actually SEE the flavor!

STRAWBERRY - NUT BREAD

20-25 minutes to prepare *1 hour to bake*

This refreshing, moist bread is good enough to be served by itself, or with a fresh cup of tea. The combination of sweet strawberries and crunchy nuts, make this bread the perfect treat to serve when you have guests in for the weekend (it'll give them something to nibble on).

2	cups all-purpose flour	1	cup mashed strawberries, including juice
2	teaspoons baking powder	1	egg
1/2	teaspoon baking soda	2	tablespoons butter, melted
1/4	teaspoon salt	2	tablespoons boiling water
3/4	cup granulated sugar	1/2	cup crushed pecans or walnuts

Preheat oven to 350 degrees. Sift together the dry ingredients into a large bowl and make a well in the center. In a separate bowl, combine the mashed strawberries, egg, melted butter and water. Mix well with a wire whisk. Fold in crushed nuts. Pour strawberry mixture into center of flour mixture and fold ingredients together with a wooden spoon until just combined. Pour batter into a lightly greased bread pan and bake for 40-50 minutes or until a knife comes out clean. Cool on rack before removing bread from pan.

MAKES 1 LOAF

BASIC BANANA BREAD

15-20 minutes to prepare   *1 hour to bake*

This is the basic banana bread recipe; one known and loved by all. If you desire a little change, add walnuts or chocolate chips. You basically can't go wrong with this bread, everyone enjoys it.

- **2 cups all-purpose flour**
- **2 teaspoons baking powder**
- **1/2 teaspoon baking soda**
- **1/2 teaspoon salt**
- **3 large, overripe bananas***
- **1 egg**
- **3/4 cup granulated sugar**
- **1/4 cup buttermilk**
- **1/4 teaspoon lemon rind**

Preheat oven to 350 degrees. Sift together the flour, baking powder, baking soda and salt into a large bowl, make a well in the center and set aside. In a separate bowl, mash bananas until mushy and add egg. Mix with a wire whisk until well blended. Add sugar, buttermilk and lemon rind and mix well. Pour banana mixture into center of flour mixture and fold together with a wooden spoon until just blended. Pour batter into a lightly greased bread pan and bake for 1 hour, or until a knife comes out virtually clean. Cool on rack before removing from pan. Serve warm or cold.

*It is important that the bananas be overripe and somewhat mushy. Underripe bananas will not perform as well in this recipe.

MAKES 1 LOAF

ORANGE BREAD

15-20 minutes to prepare *1 hour to bake*

This is a perfect afternoon bread, or a bread for company. The zest and fresh taste of orange make this a refreshing, appetizing treat. In fact, if it wasn't for the shape, you might think you were eating cake.

1 1/2	cups all-purpose flour	2	eggs
1	teaspoon baking powder	1	tablespoon orange juice
1/2	teaspoon salt	1	tablespoon grated orange rind
3/4	cup granulated sugar	1/2	cup milk
4	tablespoons butter		

Glaze:

2	tablespoons orange juice, heated	1/2	cup confectioners sugar

Preheat oven to 350 degrees. Sift together the flour, baking powder and salt, set aside. In a large mixing bowl, beat together the butter and sugar until creamy. Add eggs and mix well. Beat in milk, orange juice and orange rind. Gradually add flour mixture and mix until smooth. Pour batter into a lightly greased bread pan and bake for 1 hour, or until a knife comes out clean. Remove bread from oven and cool on rack 10 minutes before removing loaf from pan. Combine warm orange juice and confectioners sugar in a small bowl and mix with a wire whisk until smooth. Remove bread from pan and place on a sheet of wax paper. While still warm, pour the glaze over the bread and allow streams of the glaze to run down the sides. Cool before serving.

MAKES 1 LOAF

SPICED LEMON BREAD

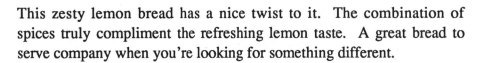

20-25 minutes to prepare   *1 hour to bake*

This zesty lemon bread has a nice twist to it. The combination of spices truly compliment the refreshing lemon taste. A great bread to serve company when you're looking for something different.

2 1/4	cups all-purpose flour	1/4	teaspoon ground ginger
2	teaspoons baking powder	1/2	cup (1 stick) butter, melted
1/4	teaspoon salt	2/3	cup milk
1/2	cup granulated sugar	2	eggs, lightly beaten
1	teaspoon ground cinnamon	1	tablespoon fresh lemon juice
1/4	teaspoon ground nutmeg	1/4	teaspoon grated fresh lemon rind

Glaze:

2	teaspoons lemon juice	2/3	cup confectioners sugar

Preheat oven to 350 degrees. Sift together into a large bowl the flour, baking powder, salt, sugar, cinnamon, nutmeg and ginger. Make a well in he center of the mixture and set aside. In a small mixing bowl, combine butter, milk, eggs, lemon juice and lemon rind and mix well with a wire whisk. Pour mixture into the center of the flour mixture and mix well with a wooden spoon or spatula until combined. Pour batter into a lightly greased bread pan and bake for 1 hour or until a knife comes out clean. Cool on rack for at least 10 minutes before removing loaf from pan. Place bread on a large piece of wax paper. Warm the lemon juice in the microwave or in a small sauce pan and add the confectioners sugar, blend with a wire whisk until smooth. Pour mixture over the bread with a spoon, allowing streams of the glaze to run down the sides. Cool slightly and remove from wax paper before serving.

MAKES 1 LOAF

BUTTERMILK BISCUITS

10-15 minutes to prepare   *10-12 minutes to bake*

As tempting as it may be to buy pre-made biscuits, these light, flaky biscuits are simple to prepare and you'll be proud to call them your own.

3   **tablespoons butter**
1 1/2   **cups all-purpose flour**
1 1/2   **teaspoons baking powder**
1/2   **teaspoon baking soda**
1/4   **teaspoon salt**
1/2   **cup plus 2 tablespoons buttermilk**

Place 2 tablespoons of the butter in a cast iron skillet and place in a 500 degree oven to preheat while you prepare the biscuits. In a large bowl, combine the flour, baking powder, baking soda and salt. Mix together with a fork and make a well in the center. Melt the remaining tablespoon of butter and combine with buttermilk. Pour buttermilk mixture into the center of the well and fold ingredients together with a wooden spoon or spatula. Once a manageable dough has formed, turn to a lightly floured surface and knead briefly, about 1 minute. Using the heal of your hand, press dough out until it is about 1/2" thick. Cut out 6-7 biscuits with an upside down glass. Combine leftover scraps and roll out again for more biscuits if necessary. Remove skillet from oven and place biscuits in hot butter. Turn over once and return skillet to oven. Bake biscuits for 10-12 minutes or until puffed up and golden brown. Serve warm.

MAKES ABOUT 6-8 BISCUITS

PERFECT POPOVERS

5-10 minutes to prepare   *35 minutes to bake*

These popovers are so easy to make that you can prepare them at the last minute, when you realize you need something extra. The ingredients are probably already in your kitchen, making this the ideal side dish for almost any meal. Serve with soups, stews, juicy meat or chicken dishes, breakfast, and virtually all other occasions when a light, fluffy popover is desired.

2 **eggs**
1 **cup all-purpose flour**
1/2 **teaspoon salt**
1 **cup cold milk**

Preheat oven to 450 degrees. Beat eggs with a wire whisk in a large bowl. Sift in flour and salt. Add milk and mix with a wire whisk until most of the lumps are gone. Pour batter into lightly greased muffin tins until 2/3 full. Bake for 15 minutes, reduce heat to 350 degrees and continue baking for 20 minutes. Cool on wire racks before serving.

HINT: To prevent popovers from collapsing while cooling, pierce the top of each one with a sharp knife to allow steam to escape.

MAKES ABOUT 8-10 MUFFINS

VARIATION: For cheese flavored popovers, prepare popovers above, spoon 2 tablespoons of batter into each muffin tin, sprinkle with 1 teaspoon of Parmesan cheese each, and cover with 1 more tablespoon of batter. Bake as directed.

CINNAMON/RAISIN BAGELS

10-15 minutes to prepare   *35 minutes to stand*   *40-45 minutes to boil and bake*

You can't imagine the response you get when you tell people you've made home-made bagels. Surprisingly, they are not that difficult to prepare. The most time consuming aspect of these tasty morsels, is the time allowed for the dough to rise. If you have the time, its well worth the wait!

1 1/2	cups warm water
2	packets dry active yeast
5	tablespoons granulated sugar
1	tablespoon salt
1	tablespoon cinnamon
4	cups all-purpose flour
1	cup raisins

Dissolve yeast in warm water. Stir in 3 tablespoons of the sugar, salt, cinnamon, raisins and flour. (If 4 cups is not enough to make a stiff dough, add more until it does.) Turn to a lightly floured surface and knead for 10 minutes. Cover with a dish towel and let stand at room temperature for 15 minutes. Divide dough into 12 equal parts, roll each into a ball and using your finger, punch a 1" hole in the center. Place on an ungreased cookie sheet, cover with a dish towel and let stand for 20 minutes. In a large pot, bring 4 quarts of water and the remaining sugar to a boil. Reduce heat to simmer and add bagels four at a time. Simmer two minutes on each side and remove. Continue until all bagels have been boiled. Place bagels on a lightly greased baking sheet and bake at 375 degrees for 25-30 minutes, or until lightly browned.

VARIATION: replace 2 cups of the white flour with whole wheat flour.

MAKES 1 DOZEN BAGELS

Vegetable Side Dishes

VEGETABLE MEDLEY

10-15 minutes preparation and cooking time

When you find yourself unable to decide which vegetables to serve with your main course, try this medley of a few different vegetables. The combination is lovely, and the variation in colors adds a nice touch to any dinner plate.

1-2 **tablespoons sweet, unsalted butter**
  1 **small onion, sliced**
  2 **carrots, peeled and julienned**
  1 **medium zucchini, julienned**
  1 **medium ripe tomato. sliced**
      Salt and ground black pepper to taste

Heat butter in a large skillet over medium heat. Add onion and saute until tender, about 3-5 minutes. Add carrots and zucchini and stir to coat vegetables with butter. Cover and saute over low heat until tender crisp, about 8-10 minutes, stirring occasionally. Stir in tomatoes and heat through. Season with salt and pepper and serve.

SERVES 2

TOMATO AND ZUCCHINI SAUTE

10 minutes to prepare

30 minutes to cook

This zesty vegetable side dish is a wonderful complement to many main dishes. It goes extremely well with most beef and chicken dishes. Also, this dish does a wonderful job in adding color to an otherwise bland looking plate!

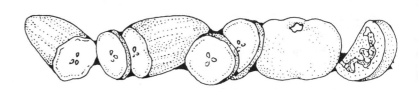

 1   tablespoon olive or vegetable oil
 1   small onion, chopped
 2   large tomatoes, chopped
1/2   teaspoon salt
 1   teaspoon chopped fresh basil, or 1/2 teaspoon dried
1/4   teaspoon oregano
1/4   cup dry white wine
1/4   teaspoon black pepper
 2   medium zucchini, unpeeled and sliced 1/4" thick

Heat oil in a large skillet over medium heat. Add onion and saute until tender, about 3-5 minutes. Stir in tomatoes, salt, basil, oregano, wine and pepper. Bring to a boil. Cover, reduce heat and simmer for 20 minutes. Add zucchini and simmer over medium heat, stirring frequently, until sauce thickens and reduces, about 8-10 minutes. Serve hot.

SERVES 2-3

ZESTY ZUCCHINI

10-15 minutes preparation and cooking time

For anyone who is not an avid fan of zucchini, I suggest you try this dish. The combination of flavors creates a mouth-watering assemble that is sure to change your mind about zucchini forever.

1-2	tablespoons butter or margarine
1/4	teaspoon dried basil
1/4	teaspoon salt
1/4	teaspoon ground black pepper
	Dash of Tabasco or other hot sauce
1	medium zucchini, sliced 1/4" thick
2	tablespoons grated Parmesan cheese

Heat butter in a large skillet over medium heat. Add basil, salt, pepper and hot sauce and mix well. Add zucchini and saute until tender, about 3-5 minutes. Add cheese and continue cooking until zucchini is golden brown. Serve.

SERVES 2

GREEN BEANS WITH BASIL AND TOMATOES

15 minutes preparation and cooking time

This simple side dish is a tasty variation to the ordinary plain beans. The basil and tomato add a zesty, fresh taste, and make this side dish a perfect match for any entree.

1/2 lb. green beans, ends trimmed	2 small tomatoes, cut into wedges
1 tablespoon butter or margarine	1 tablespoon chopped onion
1 teaspoon chopped fresh basil, or 1/2 teaspoon dried	Salt and black pepper to taste

Steam green beans in a saucepan or in the microwave until tender crisp, about 5 minutes. In large skillet, melt the butter over medium heat. Stir in basil, onion and tomato. Simmer over low heat until tender, about 5 minutes. Stir in green beans and season with salt and pepper. Serve immediately.

SERVES 2

CARROTS WITH A TWIST

10-15 minutes to prepare   *15 minutes to bake*

Carrots seem to have an affinity with sour cream and horseradish. Try it for yourself and discover a completely different tasting carrot.

3-4	medium carrots	1/3	cup sour cream
2	tablespoons minced onion	1/4	teaspoon salt
2	tablespoons horseradish	1/4	teaspoon pepper

Preheat oven to 375 degrees. Peel carrots and cut diagonally into large slices. Place in a large sauce pan and add enough cold water to just cover the carrots. Bring to a boil and cook until tender, about 6-8 minutes. Drain carrots, reserving 1/4 cup of the liquid from the pan. Place carrots in a 2 quart baking dish (or smaller one if you have it). In a separate bowl, combine reserved liquid, onion, horseradish, sour cream, salt and pepper. Mix well and pour mixture over carrots. Cover and bake for 15 minutes. Serve.

SERVES 2

PEAS AND CARROTS

10-15 minutes preparation and cooking time

You CAN buy premixed peas and carrots in a box—but WHY when homemade vegetable combinations taste so much better?!

3-4	carrots, peeled and sliced diagonally into chunks
8 oz.	package frozen young peas, thawed and drained
2	tablespoons fresh dill, minced, or 1 tablespoon dried dill weed
1	tablespoon fresh lemon juice
1	tablespoon butter or margarine
	Salt and ground black pepper to taste

Steam carrots in a colander placed over a 1-2" of boiling water (or in the microwave) until tender crisp, about 4-6 minutes. In a large bowl, combine carrots, peas, lemon juice and dill and toss well. Heat butter in a large skillet and add vegetables. Season with salt and pepper and saute over medium heat until heated through. Serve warm.

SERVES 2-3

BROCCOLI WITH WARM VINAIGRETTE

10-15 minutes preparation and cooking time

This zesty creation adds a nice twist to ordinary broccoli. It doesn't take long to prepare, so if you've got the time to steam the broccoli, you've got the time to enhance it with a combination of hard boiled eggs and a flavorful warm vinaigrette.

- 2 cups fresh broccoli florets
- 2 slices bacon, cooked in skillet or microwave until crisp
- 1 tablespoon butter or margarine
- 2 tablespoons chopped red onion
- 2 tablespoons lemon juice
- 2 tablespoons red wine vinegar
- 1 teaspoon Dijon mustard
- 1 tablespoon water
- 1/4 teaspoon black pepper
- 1 egg, hard boiled

Blanche broccoli in a large pot of boiling water for 1-2 minutes, until tender crisp. In a small sauce pan, saute onion in butter until tender. Break up bacon slices into little pieces and add to onions. Add lemon juice, vinegar, mustard, water and pepper and mix well. Simmer over medium-low heat for 2-3 minutes. Place broccoli on serving plate or on individual plates. Chop egg into tiny pieces and sprinkle over broccoli. Pour warm vinaigrette over broccoli and egg and serve.

SERVES 2-3

BETTER BRUSSEL SPROUTS

15 minutes preparation and cooking time

A slight variation in preparation can enhance the flavor of these brussel sprouts in just minutes.

1 lb. **fresh brussel sprouts, or 1 box frozen**
  2 **tablespoons Dijon mustard**
1/4 **teaspoon salt**
1/4 **teaspoon black pepper**

If using fresh brussel sprouts, discard the outer leaves and cut off the thick fibrous ends. Place sprouts in a large pot of lightly salted boiling water and boil for 6-7 minutes, until tender. Drain and set aside. In a large skillet, combine the mustard, salt and pepper. Heat over low heat until heated through. Add brussel sprouts to skillet and stir gently with a fork until sprouts are coated with mixture. Serve immediately.

SERVES 2

SPINACH AND POTATO MEDLEY

15-20 minutes preparation and cooking time

This recipe combines two great tasting vegetables to create an ensemble that's irresistible. Serve this dish with virtually all meat and poultry dishes. It's a simple recipe that will make any meal complete.

1   **package frozen spinach, thawed and drained**
2   **slices bacon, cooked until crisp**
1   **tablespoon butter or margarine**
1   **small onion, chopped**
4   **small new red potatoes**
     Salt and ground black pepper to taste

Wash potatoes and remove any black knots. Place in a large pot of cold, lightly salted water. Bring to a boil, reduce heat and simmer (water should be almost still) until tender, about 8-10 minutes. Remove from pot and set aside to cool. In a large skillet, melt butter over medium heat. Add onion and saute until tender. Add spinach and mix well. Slice potatoes into large chunks and add to spinach mixture. Break up bacon into little bits and add to skillet. Season with salt and pepper and heat through. Serve.

SERVES 2-3

CHEESY POTATOES

10 minutes to prepare   *1 hour to cook*

The most appealing feature of this side dish is that it can be left alone while it cooks. Except for a few stirs every now and then, you are free to prepare the rest of your meal, or just relax. These potatoes are an excellent side dish for barbecued chicken and many meat dishes, as long as they don't contain heavy cream sauces.

4	large potatoes, sliced 1/8 inch thick
1	small onion, chopped
1 1/2	cups milk
1/2	tablespoon butter or margarine
1/2	teaspoon salt
1	tablespoon chopped fresh parsley or 1 teaspoon dried
1/8	teaspoon pepper
2	tablespoons ketchup
1/2	teaspoon Worcestershire sauce
3/4	cup American cheese, chopped

Combine all ingredients in a heavy skillet. Cook over low heat, stirring occasionally, for 1 hour or until potatoes are tender.

SERVES 2-4

NEW POTATOES WITH HERB SEASONING

5-10 minutes to prepare   *40 minutes to bake*

These potatoes look and taste great. By allowing the potatoes to bake in a thin coating, a crispy, more flavorful potato emerges from the oven. A perfect compliment to all meat and poultry dishes.

> 4 **small new red potatoes**
> 2 **tablespoons butter or margarine, melted**
> 3 **tablespoons all-purpose flour**
> 1/2 **teaspoon black pepper**
> 1/2 **teaspoon salt**
> 1 **teaspoon dried parsley**

Preheat oven to 450 degrees. Wash potatoes and remove any black knots from outer skin. Peel a 1/2" band around the center of each potato. Combine all dry ingredients in a small bowl. Brush peeled potatoes lightly with melted butter and roll in flour mixture until well coated. Place in a lightly greased shallow baking dish, cover with foil and bake for 40 minutes, or until potatoes are tender on the inside and crispy on the outside.

SERVES 2

PARSLEY RICE

5-10 minutes to prepare   *35-40 minutes to bake*

This is a perfect side dish for virtually all main courses. It goes beautifully with ham, many beef dishes as well as fish and poultry. It's a well-seasoned, versatile side dish created for those times when you're looking for something different.

1 1/2	cups white rice, uncooked
2	cups water
1/2	cup milk
1	egg, beaten
1	tablespoon onion, chopped
2	tablespoons fresh parsley, chopped
1/2	teaspoon Worcestershire sauce
1/2	teaspoon salt
1/4	cup sharp Cheddar cheese, grated

Preheat oven to 350 degrees. Combine all ingredients but the cheese in a large bowl and mix well. Pour mixture into a 2 quart casserole dish and top with grated Cheddar cheese. Cover and bake for 35-40 minutes. Rice is ready when liquid is absorbed and mixture is set. Serve immediately.

SERVES 2-4

ITALIAN RICE

30 minutes preparation and cooking time

I call this "Italian Rice" because it goes beautifully with almost all Italian dishes, especially veal and chicken. It's simple to prepare so be sure to add this to your next Italian dinner for two.

1	cup white rice, uncooked
2	cups water
1	tablespoon butter or margarine
1/2	teaspoon salt
1/4	teaspoon black pepper
1/2	teaspoon oregano
1/4	cup Parmesan cheese, grated
1/3	cup milk

Melt butter in a large skillet and add rice. Saute over medium heat until rice is golden brown, stirring constantly. Add water, salt, pepper and oregano, cover and simmer until water is absorbed and rice is fluffy, about 20 minutes. While rice is cooking, scald milk in a small sauce pan. Stir cheese and milk into rice mixture just before serving. Heat through and serve.

SERVES 2

TOMATOES WITH BASIL-MUSTARD VINAIGRETTE

10-15 minutes to prepare

This light, refreshing side dish adds the perfect zing to any meal. Served as an appetizer over Romaine or red lettuce, or served with the main course, this dish is the ideal companion for virtually anything. In addition, the vinaigrette can be made in advance and refrigerated until ready to use.

BASIL

3-4   large ripe tomatoes, cut into wedges
1/4   cup fresh basil, minced
1   tablespoon Dijon mustard
1/4   cup red wine vinegar
1   tablespoon olive oil
3   tablespoons water
   Black pepper to taste

In a food processor fitted with the metal blade or a blender combine the basil, mustard and vinegar. Process until well blended. While machine is running, gradually add oil and then water. Process until thoroughly blended. Add pepper to taste. Pour vinaigrette over tomato wedges and serve.

SERVES 2

SAUTEED TOMATOES

10-15 minutes to prepare

Looking for an easy, yet slightly different variation to a tomato side dish? This recipe enhances the delicious flavor of the tomato and adds a splash of color to any dish. Serve with any meat, poultry or fish dish.

1-2 tablespoons butter or margarine
2-3 large, ripe tomatoes
1/4 teaspoon marjoram or oregano
Pinch of sugar
Salt and ground black pepper to taste

Skin tomatoes: Slice a large X at the base of each tomato. Spear the stem end with a fork and immerse each tomato into rapidly boiling water for 10 seconds. Remove from water and peel skin off with ease. Halve each tomato and remove the seeds with a small spoon. Cut each tomato into bite-size chunks. In a large skillet, melt butter over medium high heat and add the tomatoes. Saute over medium heat for 3-4 minutes, or until juices start to flow. Sprinkle with sugar, marjoram, salt and pepper and heat through. Serve warm.

SERVES 2

TOMATO AND CORN SALAD

10 minutes to prepare   *at least 4 hours to chill*

Because this recipe must be refrigerated before serving, it's an ideal salad to prepare in advance. It's a refreshing, flavorful combination of tomatoes and corn that can be served with meat, poultry or fish.

3-4	Italian plum tomatoes, sliced into 6-8 pieces each
1	cup fresh or frozen sweet corn, thawed and drained
1/2	small red onion, chopped
2	tablespoons fresh parsley, minced
1	teaspoon fresh basil, chopped
1/2	teaspoon salt
1/4	teaspoon ground black pepper
1	tablespoon fresh lemon juice
1	tablespoon olive or vegetable oil
1	tablespoon red wine vinegar

Combine all ingredients in a large bowl and toss well. Refrigerate at least 4 hours before serving. Serve over red or Romaine lettuce.

SERVES 2-3

STUFFED TOMATOES

20-25 minutes to prepare   *22-24 minutes total baking time*

For an elegant side dish packed with flavor, prepare this zesty tomato surprise. You'll be amazed how easy it is to prepare such an impressive looking vegetable!

2-3	large ripe tomatoes
1	teaspoon vegetable oil
1	clove garlic, minced
2	tablespoons chopped onion
1	small zucchini, chopped
1/2	cup broccoli florets
1	carrot, chopped
1/2	cup Orzo pasta
2	tablespoons tomato paste
1	teaspoon soy sauce
1/2	teaspoon dried basil
1/2	teaspoon dried thyme
1/4	teaspoon dried parsley
1/4	teaspoon salt
1/4	teaspoon ground black pepper
1	tablespoon dried bread crumbs
1	tablespoon grated Parmesan cheese

Preheat oven to 350 degrees. (If you have a food processor fitted with the metal blade, it is easiest to chop all vegetables into small pieces, uniform in size. If not, coarsely chop with a sharp knife and set aside.) Cut off the tops of each tomato and spoon out the seeds and core, being careful not to tear the outside skin. Place on a baking sheet, upside down and bake for 7-10 minutes, or until tender (do not cook until mushy). Remove from oven and increase oven temperature to 375 degrees. Cook Orzo according to package directions, using the minimum suggested cooking time. Rinse under cold water, drain and set aside. In a large skillet, heat the oil and add onion and garlic. Saute over medium heat until tender, about 3 minutes. Add zucchini, broccoli and carrot and saute until tender crisp, about 3 more minutes. Stir in cooked Orzo, tomato paste, soy sauce, basil, thyme, parsley, salt and pepper. Simmer until heated through and remove from heat. Cool a few minutes before stuffing tomatoes. Fill tomatoes evenly with mixture, pressing down slightly to pack in mixture. Sprinkle the top with a mixture of the bread crumbs and Parmesan cheese. Place on baking sheet and bake for 12-15 minutes, or until heated through and golden brown on top. Serve immediately.

SERVES 2-3

STUFFED GREEN PEPPERS

10-15 minutes to prepare   *27-30 minutes total baking time*

When a dish is served with a savory stuffed pepper as the side dish, a certain look is created. A look that reveals that someone has taken the time to create an extra-special meal. Well, this vegetable side dish has that extra-special look, without requiring the extra time.

2	medium green bell peppers
1/2	teaspoon marjoram or oregano
2	tablespoons fresh parsley, chopped
1	small onion, minced
1	cup cooked white rice
1	tablespoon lemon juice
1/4	teaspoon ground black pepper
2	tablespoons chopped Pimento
1/4	cup Cheddar cheese, grated

Preheat oven to 325. Cut off the tops of each pepper and discard. Remove seeds and core from the inside of each pepper. Stand peppers on a baking sheet (if the peppers don't stand, slice a thin piece from the bottom to make a flat surface). Bake for 12-15 minutes, or until tender but not wilted. In a large bowl, combine all remaining ingredients but the cheese and mix well. Stuff the peppers evenly with the rice mixture and return to baking sheet. Cover the top of each pepper with grated cheese and return peppers to oven. Bake for 15 minutes, until golden. Serve immediately.

SERVES 2

PASTA SALAD

15-20 minutes to prepare   *30 minutes to chill*

Pasta salad is always a treat in the warm summer months. This recipe not only tastes delicious with hamburgers or chicken on the grill, but makes a light, refreshing meal in itself.

1/2 **lb. spiral or tri-color noodles**
  2 **tablespoons coarsely chopped red onion**
  1 **medium red pepper, roasted* and sliced**
  2 **carrots, sliced diagonally into chunks**
  1 **cup broccoli florets**
1/3 **cup sour cream**
  1 **cup plain yogurt**
  1 **tablespoon Dijon mustard**
  2 **tablespoons fresh parsley, chopped**
  1 **teaspoon fresh dill, or 1/2 teaspoon dried**
1/2 **teaspoon salt**
1/4 **teaspoon black pepper**
   Dash of paprika

Blanche broccoli in a large pot of rapidly boiling water for 1 minute. Drain, rinse under cold water and set aside. Cook pasta according to package directions, drain and run under cold water to prevent further cooking. In a large bowl, combine sour cream, yogurt, mustard, parsley, dill, salt, pepper and paprika. Stir in warm pasta and mix well. Add broccoli and remaining vegetables and toss. Chill at least 30 minutes before serving (if you must chill salad more than 30 minutes and mixture seems to have dried out, add more sour cream or yogurt as necessary to "spruce" it up).

SERVES 2-4

*To roast red pepper, spear it on one end with a fork and hold it over high heat of a gas or electric stove. When outside skin is charred, place pepper in a sealed container for 2 minutes to steam. Remove from container and gently pull off blackened skin with your fingers. Use pepper as directed in recipe.

NOTE: Preroasted peppers can be found by the jar in most supermarkets.

ESSIE'S PARTY POTATO SALAD

45-55 minutes preparation and cooking time

This will be the best potato salad you have ever tasted. Essie is notorious for bringing her potato salad to picnics and parties (and if she doesn't—look out)! The recipe is very large, making it the perfect salad for entertaining. If you don't need a large batch of potato salad, cut the recipe in half—and enjoy!

10	lbs. small new red potatoes
6-8	eggs, hard boiled
2-3	carrots, grated
2 1/4	cups mayonnaise
2	tablespoons fresh lemon juice
1/2	teaspoon celery seed
1	teaspoon salt
1	teaspoon paprika (for garnish)
1	tablespoon fresh parsley (for garnish)

Put potatoes in a large stock pot with enough water to cover and bring to a boil. Cook over high heat until potatoes are tender but still slightly firm, about 20-30 minutes (to test for doneness, a potato will fall off a fork when pricked). Drain potatoes and while still warm peel and slice into thick slices (don't cube potatoes because they will have a greater tendency to become mushy). Place potato slices into a LARGE bowl. Peel and slice 4 of the eggs and add to potatoes. Add grated carrots and mix together gently. In a small bowl, combine the mayonnaise, lemon juice, celery seed and salt. Fold mixture gently into potatoes (while the potatoes are still warm) and mix well. Slice the remaining 2 eggs. Sprinkle the top of the salad with paprika and parsley, garnish the edges with egg slices and serve.

MAKES APPROXIMATELY 10 POUNDS OF POTATO SALAD

 **9**

Desserts & Treats For Someone Special

ORANGE CHOCOLATE MOUSSE

25 minutes to prepare   *2 hours to chill*

This tasty treat is a must to top off a romantic dinner for two. The tangy orange taste mixed with chocolate makes for a simply heavenly finale that is delightfully light, yet chocolatey enough to satisfy even the most severe sweet tooth.

2	oz. semisweet chocolate (two 1 oz. squares)		Dash of salt
1	oz. unsweetened chocolate (one 1 oz. square)	1/8	teaspoon Cream of Tartar
1	tablespoon light corn syrup	3	tablespoons granulated sugar
2	tablespoons frozen orange juice concentrate	3/4	cup whipping cream
3	eggs, separated	2	tablespoons fresh orange rind

Melt the two chocolates together in a the top of a double boiler, or in a small sauce pan set inside a larger pan of simmering water, or in the microwave (when using the microwave, put a small glass of water on the side). Stir the corn syrup and orange concentrate into the chocolate until smooth. Beat egg whites with salt and Cream of Tartar until soft peaks form. (Soft peaks can be distinguished when the beaters are pulled up from the egg whites and the peak folds over a bit.) Gradually add the sugar until the mixture is stiff and shiny (peaks retain their shape) and set aside. Beat egg yolks until creamy and pale. Blend yolks into chocolate mixture. Fold in a large spoonful of the egg whites, and then fold in the rest (FOLD—do not stir - or egg whites will lose their consistency). Beat 1/2 cup of whipping cream until stiff and fold into chocolate mixture. Spoon into four individual serving glasses (use the new ones you got as a wedding gift!) and chill for at least 2 hours. When ready to serve, whip the extra whipping cream until stiff and placed in dollops on top.

Sprinkle orange rind on top of whipped cream - makes for a nice presentation!

SERVES 4

CHOCOLATE DECADENCE

20-25 minutes to prepare *30 minutes to bake*

This dessert is the perfect chocolate treat that's fun to eat. The dense chocolate squares, topped with light, creamy whipped cream or vanilla ice cream, create an ensemble that's difficult to resist.

1/4 cup (1/2 stick) butter	1 teaspoon vanilla extract
4 oz. unsweetened chocolate (four 1 oz. squares)	
2 large eggs	1/4 cup buttermilk
Pinch salt	3/4 cup all-purpose flour
1 1/2 cups granulated sugar	
Chocolate shavings (or crushed Oreo cookies!)	

Preheat oven to 350 degrees. In the top of a double boiler, or in a sauce pan set inside a larger sauce pan of simmering water, melt butter and chocolate together. Remove from heat and set aside. In a large mixing bowl, beat eggs and salt for approximately 2 minutes, or until mixture is doubled in size. Gradually add sugar, beating constantly. Beat in the vanilla and buttermilk. While beating on slow speed, gradually add chocolate mixture. Remove bowl from mixer, and sift in flour. Stir with a wooden spoon until just combined. Pour batter into a lightly greased, 9" baking pan (square or round) and bake for 30 minutes or until edges pull slightly away from sides of pan and a toothpick comes out virtually clean. Cool in pan on wire rack before cutting. Cut the decadence into squares or triangles and top with whipped cream or vanilla ice cream. Sprinkle with chocolate shavings or crushed cookies and serve.

MAKES ABOUT 10-12 SQUARES

NOTE: I have found that this recipe tastes almost better the next day if refrigerated, so if you need to prepare it in advance, don't worry.

MUMMY'S CHOCOLATE PIE

15-20 minutes to prepare   *1 1/2 hours total chilling time*

An old family favorite that words cannot describe. You simply must taste it to believe it. In addition, this is an ideal make-ahead dessert, because it requires chilling time.

Graham Cracker Crust: (a pre-made crust may be substituted)

1 1/2 cups Graham cracker crumbs	6 tablespoons butter, melted
1/4 cup confectioners sugar	

Combine all ingredients in a large bowl and mix with a fork until well blended. Pour mixture into a 9" pie plate and either press down with your fingers, or press another pie pan of the same diameter firmly onto the crumbs until an even thickness of crust is produced. Chill in refrigerator while making the filling.

Filling:

6 oz. package chocolate chips	4 eggs, separated
3 tablespoons milk	1 teaspoon vanilla extract
2 tablespoons granulated sugar	1 cup heavy cream

Melt chocolate chips in a double boiler, or in a small sauce pan set in a larger sauce pan of simmering water. Stir in milk and sugar, mix well and heat through. Refrigerate chocolate mixture for 30 minutes. Beat egg whites until stiff but not dry (they are ready when beater is lifted and peaks retain shape). Remove chocolate mixture from refrigerator and whisk in egg yolks one at a time, mixing well after each addition. Add vanilla and mix well. Fold in 1 large spoonful of the egg whites, and then fold in the rest. Mix until completely blended. Pour mixture into graham cracker crust and chill until firm, about 1 hour. When ready to serve, beat heavy cream until stiff. Spread whipped cream on top of pie and serve.

MAKES 1 9" PIE

BOSTON CREAM PIE

35-45 minutes to prepare   *12-15 minutes to bake*

This recipe is another one of my mother's. The combination of moist cake layers, creamy filling and rich chocolate icing is perfect. In addition, the cake and filling can be made up to 24 hours in advance and refrigerated separately. Wait to assemble and ice the cake until just before serving.

Cake:

1 cup all-purpose flour	1 cup granulated sugar
1 1/4 teaspoons baking powder	1 1/2 tablespoons cold water
1/8 teaspoon salt	1 1/2 teaspoons lemon juice
4 large eggs, separated	1 teaspoon vanilla extract

Preheat oven to 375 degrees. Grease two 9" cake pans, dust with flour and set aside. Sift the flour 2 times before measuring and again with the baking powder and salt, set aside. Beat egg whites until stiff but not dry. Gradually fold in 1/2 cup of the sugar. In a separate bowl, beat egg yolks until pale yellow and creamy. Beat in water, lemon juice and vanilla. Beat in remaining sugar. Fold a large spoonful of egg whites into egg yolk mixture. Fold in remaining egg whites. Fold flour mixture into egg mixture and mix until completely blended. Pour batter into prepared cake pans and bake for 12-15 minutes, or until a toothpick or knife comes out clean. Cool thoroughly on wire racks.

Filling:

1 1/2 cups milk	3 egg yolks
3 tablespoons cornstarch	2 tablespoons butter, melted
2/3 cup granulated sugar	1 teaspoon vanilla extract
1/8 teaspoon salt	

In a small sauce pan, scald the milk by heating over medium heat until tiny bubbles appear around the edges. Remove from heat and set aside. In a small bowl, combine cornstarch, sugar and salt, set aside. Beat egg yolks until pale yellow and creamy. Gradually add cornstarch mixture and mix well. Mixing on slow speed, gradually add the scalded milk. Add butter and vanilla. Pour mixture into the top of a double boiler, or a sauce pan set inside a larger sauce pan of simmering water. Simmer over medium high heat until thick and mixture resembles pudding, stirring constantly with a wire whisk. Cool thoroughly before spreading between cakes.

Icing:

3 oz. **unsweetened chocolate (three 1 oz. squares)**
1 **tablespoon butter**
1/4 **cup milk**
1 **teaspoon vanilla extract**
1 lb. **confectioners sugar, sifted**

In the top of a double boiler or a small sauce pan set inside a larger sauce pan of simmering water, melt chocolate and butter over medium heat. Remove from heat and stir in milk and vanilla. Gradually add sugar, stirring constantly, until thick, creamy and smooth. Once cake has been assembled, smooth chocolate icing over top.

To Assemble:

Spread filling mixture evenly on top of one cake. Place second cake on top. Spread icing evenly on top of cake and sprinkle with a little confectioners sugar if desired.

MAKES 1 9" CAKE/PIE

"EASY AS PIE" APPLE PIE

30 minutes to prepare   *45 minutes to bake*

This recipe is an original from my mother-in-law who makes the best apple pie ever. It's easy, quick and everyone loves it. The old adage holds true in this case—"the simpler the better".

8-10   **Mackintosh apples, peeled and cut into eight slices each (skins may be left on if desired)**
1/4   **cup granulated sugar**
1   **teaspoon cinnamon**
9"   **pie shell, top and bottom (recipe follows or you may use premade uncooked crusts)**
1   **egg, slightly beaten**

Preheat oven to 375 degrees. Place one half of the pie crust in the bottom of a 9" pie plate. Press the dough down around the rim with your fingers to form a 1/2" lip hanging over the edges. Spread apples evenly into uncooked pie crust. (The apples should be higher than the rim of the pie plate because they shrink during cooking.) Sprinkle the sugar evenly over the apples. Sprinkle cinnamon over sugar and apples. Place second crust over apple filling. Press down with a fork along the rim of the dish to seal the two crusts together (if any areas are not sealed, you will have a nice mess to clean up in the oven!). Brush the surface with beaten egg. Prick several steam vents in the top with a fork to allow steam to escape during cooking. Bake for 55-60 minutes, or until golden brown and bubbling out of holes. Cool on rack before serving.

Pie Crust:

3   **cups all-purpose flour**
1   **teaspoon salt**

1   **cup (2 sticks) butter or margarine***
6   **tablespoons cold water**

*Using margarine will make the crust more mealy, rather than flaky in texture.

You might think it's easier to buy a pre-made pie crust, but this crust is very easy - and you get the added benefit of knowing you "made it from scratch"!

Sift the flour before measuring and resift again with the salt. Cut the butter into small chunks and add to flour. Cut the butter into the flour with two knives or a food processor fitted with the metal blade, until butter is pea-size and mixture resembles coarse meal. Add water one tablespoon at a time and stir with a fork or process until a manageable dough forms. Form dough into a ball with your hands and split into two slightly uneven parts. Place the larger of the two halves in the center of a pie plate and press from the center out until the crust reaches the top of the sides of the dish (you may also use a rolling pin to roll the dough out on a lightly floured surface until it is the size of an upside down pie plate). For the top crust, use the smaller portion of dough and roll from the center out, decreasing the pressure as you reach the sides so as not to taper the edges. Roll the dough until it is large enough to cover the apples.

CARROT CAKE

15 minutes to prepare *40-45 minutes to bake*

After many experiments, I have finally found what I believe to be the best carrot cake recipe ever. It is a moist, delicious cake smothered in a rich, creamy icing.

2 1/2	cups all-purpose flour	2	eggs
2	cups granulated sugar	1/2	cup (1 stick) butter, melted
1	teaspoon cinnamon	1	cup buttermilk
2	teaspoons baking soda	1	tablespoon fresh lemon juice
1	tablespoon baking powder	2	cups peeled, grated raw carrot
1/4	cup instant oatmeal		

Preheat oven to 350 degrees. Sift together into a large bowl the flour, sugar, cinnamon, baking soda and baking powder. Pour the oats on top, make a well in the center and set aside. In a medium bowl, combine eggs, butter and buttermilk. Mix well with a wire whisk. Add lemon juice and carrots and mix well. Pour mixture into the center of the flour mixture. Fold ingredients together with a wooden spoon or spatula until thoroughly combined. Pour evenly into 2 lightly greased 9" cake pans. Bake for 40-45 minutes, or until the cake pulls slightly away from the sides of the pan and a toothpick or knife comes out virtually clean. Cool in pans on wire racks 10 minutes before removing from pan. Remove cakes from pans and cool thoroughly. Spread cream cheese icing (recipe below) evenly on top of one of the layers. Place the second layer on top and ice the top and sides. Sprinkle the top of the cake with leftover carrot shavings and powdered sugar if desired.

Icing:

8	oz. cream cheese (low-fat if desired)	1	teaspoon vanilla extract
3/4	cup plain yogurt	1	lb. confectioners sugar

Combine all ingredients in a small mixing bowl or food processor fitted with the metal blade and blend until creamy. Smooth over carrot cake as directed.

BEST POUND CAKE IN THE WORLD

15-20 minutes to prepare   *1 1/2 hours to bake*

In a recipe list compiled by my mother, this was one of the treasures. She was absolutely correct in labeling it the "BEST".

  2   **cups all-purpose flour**
1/2 **teaspoon nutmeg**
  1   **cup (2 sticks) butter**
1 2/3 **cups granulated sugar**
  5   **eggs**
  1   **teaspoon vanilla extract**

Preheat oven to 325 degrees. Line the bottom of a lightly greased, 9" bread pan with wax paper and set aside. Sift together flour and nutmeg and set aside. In a large mixing bowl, beat together the butter and sugar until creamy. Add eggs, one at a time, mixing well after each addition. Gradually add flour, and mix well. Blend in vanilla. Pour mixture into bread pan and bake for 1 1/2 hours or until golden on top and a knife inserted into the center comes out clean. Cool in pan on wire rack before serving.

NOTE: This cake freezes very well. My mother forgot about one and found it in the freezer 1 year after she put it in. It was great!

MAKES 1 LOAF

CHOCOLATE CAKE

What would a "Newlywed Cookbook" be without the basic chocolate cake? Everyone with a sweet tooth will adore this chocolate delight. I have kept the recipe simple for you first-time cake bakers.

- 4 oz. unsweetened chocolate (four 1 oz. squares)
- 2 1/2 cups all-purpose flour
- 2 teaspoons baking soda
- 1/4 teaspoon salt
- 1/2 cup (1 stick) butter
- 1 3/4 packed cups light brown sugar
- 3 large eggs
- 2 teaspoons vanilla extract
- 1 1/2 cups buttermilk
- 1 cup boiling water

Preheat oven to 350 degrees. Prepare two 9" cake pans by buttering them or using a vegetable cooking spray and dusting with flour; set aside. In the top of a double boiler or in a small sauce pan set inside a larger sauce pan of simmering water, melt chocolate over medium heat. Remove from heat and set aside to cool. Combine the flour, baking soda and salt in a bowl, mix well with a fork or whisk and set aside. In a large mixing bowl, combine the butter and sugar and beat until blended. Add eggs, one at a time, mixing well after each addition. Beat in vanilla. While mixing on slow speed, gradually add the chocolate. Gradually add the flour mixture and buttermilk, alternating a few tablespoons of each at a time, ending with the flour mixture. Mix until just combined—DO NOT overmix or the cake will be dry. Gradually add the boiling water and mix well. Pour mixture immediately into the cake pans and bake for 30-35 minutes or until a knife comes out clean (for a supermoist cake the knife or toothpick may have a few bits of the cake clinging to it). Cool in pan on rack slightly before removing cakes from pan. Cool completely on wire racks before icing.

Icing:

4   oz. unsweetened chocolate (four 1 oz. squares)
1/2   cup (1 stick) butter
1/2   cup milk
1 lb.   confectioners sugar
2   teaspoons vanilla extract
1   teaspoon fresh orange rind

In the top of a double boiler or in a small sauce pan set inside a larger sauce pan of simmering water, melt chocolate and butter together, stirring constantly. Remove from heat and gradually add the milk, mixing well with a wire whisk. Add vanilla and orange rind. Sift in the sugar and mix well with a wooden spoon or spatula until smooth. Spread on cake while still slightly warm, the icing will harden a bit as it cools.

MAKES ONE 9" DOUBLE-LAYER CAKE

APPLE CAKE

15-20 minutes to prepare   *25 minutes to bake*

I wasn't sure whether or not to call this a cake. It requires half the work of a regular cake and looks almost like a fruit filled tart. Whatever you want to call it—you'll love it. While the savory combination bakes, the bottom layer of dough works its way between the apple slices, creating a deliciously different dessert.

1 3/4	cups all-purpose flour	1 1/2	tablespoons butter
1 1/2	teaspoons baking powder	1	egg white
1/2	teaspoon baking soda	1/2	teaspoon vanilla extract
1/4	teaspoon salt	1/2	cup buttermilk
2	tablespoons granulated sugar		
3	cups apples, pared, cored and sliced into thin slices		

Topping:

1/4	cup granulated sugar	1	teaspoon cinnamon
1 1/2	tablespoons butter, melted		

Preheat oven to 425 degrees. Sift the flour before measuring and sift again with the baking powder, baking soda, salt and sugar. Pour mixture into mixing bowl or food processor fitted with the metal blade. Cut butter into small chunks and add to flour mixture. Work butter into flour with two knives or process until mixture resembles coarse meal. Combine egg white, vanilla and buttermilk and mix well with a wire whisk. Gradually add liquid mixture to flour mixture and work in with a fork or process until a manageable dough forms, adding more flour if necessary. Place dough in a 9" square or round cake pan and press down with floured fingers until it is evenly distributed. Press apples into dough, making overlapping rows, until dough is covered. In a small bowl, combine the 1/4 cup sugar, melted butter and cinnamon and mix well. Using a knife or small spatula, spread mixture on top of apple slices. Bake for 25 minutes, or until a toothpick inserted into the center comes out clean. Cool slightly before serving.

MAKES 1 9" CAKE

APPLE STRUDEL

15-20 minutes to prepare   *30 minutes to bake*

This strudel recipe is not only a fabulous desert, but is just as incredible for breakfast, or late afternoon snack. Using pre-made puff pastry enables you to prepare this dish in minutes and tastes as tantalizingly sweet and delicate as if it was made from scratch.

  1 **uncooked puff pastry sheet (may be found in the frozen foods section of most supermarkets)**

Filling:

  6 **medium size tart apples (i.e., Mackintosh), peeled and coarsely chopped**

1/4 **cup granulated sugar**

  1 **teaspoon lemon juice**

1/2 **teaspoon lemon rind**

    Cinnamon

    Confectioners sugar

Unfold puff pastry and lay flat on a counter top. In a small bowl, combine the apples, sugar, lemon juice and lemon rind and toss until blended. Spread filling evenly on surface of pastry. Sprinkle cinnamon evenly on top of apple mixture. Gently roll up pastry (do not roll up tightly because pastry expands during cooking). Brush the top with butter and bake for 20 minutes. Reduce heat to 350 degrees, brush more butter on the surface and bake for 10 more minutes, until golden brown. Remove from oven and cool slightly. Sprinkle with confectioners sugar and serve.

MAKES 1 PUFF PASTRY—ABOUT 8-10 SLICES

APPLE TART

10 minutes to prepare   *15-17 minutes to bake*

This dessert is the perfect dish to serve when you need a quick, easy, yummy dessert for entertaining. When you invite quests over for dinner on a week night, you hardly have time to bake a cake. However, you CAN create this simple dessert and your guests will be amazed at how quickly you whipped up such a tasty number.

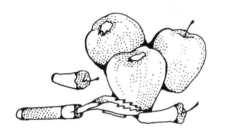

1	cup unpeeled, diced tart apples, (i.e., Mackintosh)
1	egg
3/4	cup granulated sugar
1/2	cup all-purpose flour
1	teaspoon baking powder
1/4	teaspoon cinnamon
	Pinch salt
	Dash nutmeg
1/2	cup chopped walnuts or pecans

Preheat oven to 400 degrees. In a large bowl beat together the egg and sugar with a wire whisk. Add flour, baking powder, cinnamon, salt and nutmeg. Mix well. Add apples and nuts and stir with a wooden spoon or spatula until well combined. Pour mixture into a lightly greased 8 or 9" pie pan and bake for 15-17 minutes, or until golden brown. Cool on wire rack slightly before slicing. Serve with whipped cream or ice cream, if desired.

MAKES ONE 9" TART

MOM-MOM'S FAMOUS RICE PUDDING

20-25 minutes to prepare   *5-10 minutes to bake*

This recipe came straight from the kitchen of Evelyn Blum, a friend and grandmother of my Maid-of-Honor. For years, Evelyn kept this recipe a secret from friends, children and grandchildren, all who begged for it unrelentingly. Somehow, I became fortunate enough to be let in on the secret. Once passed along to you, it can become a secret in your family for generations to come.

1	**cup uncooked white rice**
2	**cups water**
	Pinch of salt
2	**tablespoons granulated sugar, more to taste**
1	**cup milk**
1/2	**lb. cream cheese**
1	**teaspoon vanilla extract**
3	**eggs, separated**

Preheat oven to 350 degrees. In a small sauce pan, combine rice, water, salt and sugar. Simmer over medium heat until rice is soft, about 15 minutes (water does not need to be completely absorbed). Slowly add milk, stirring constantly with a wooden spoon or spatula. Stir until mixture is soft and creamy. Add cream cheese, vanilla and, if desired, more sugar to taste. Add egg yolks to rice mixture and mix well. In a small mixing bowl, beat egg whites until stiff. Fold into rice mixture. Pour into a 2 quart casserole dish and bake for 8-10 minutes, or until set. Serve warm or chilled.

SERVES 4

GRANDMOM'S EASY ORANGE SHERBET

5 minutes to prepare   *2-3 hours to chill*

This amazingly easy recipe for orange sherbet is incredible. It is my grandmother's creation, one she has learned to appreciate on those hot afternoons in Florida.

2   **cups lowfat milk**
1 1/3   **cups orange juice**
2/3   **cup granulated sugar**

Combine all ingredients in a large mixing bowl or food processor and blend until sugar is dissolved. Pour mixture in a clean bowl and place in freezer to harden. When mixture is frozen (it will probably take a couple of hours), remove from freezer and process in a food processor fitted with the metal blade or a blender until creamy. Return to freezer and chill until set.

SERVES 3-4

SUPER-EASY APPLE MUFFINS

35 minutes to prepare   *20 minutes to bake*

If your mother-in-law is notorious for baking cookies when she knows your coming, leaving you with no baking ideas of your own, next time arrive with these melt-in-your-mouth muffins that are sure to please the whole family!

1 3/4 cups raisin bran cereal, any brand
1 1/4 cups all-purpose flour
  1/2 cup granulated sugar (use 1/8 cup more if raisin
      bran does NOT have sugar in it)
1 1/2 teaspoons baking soda
  1/4 teaspoon salt
  3/4 cup buttermilk
  1/4 cup (1/2 stick) butter or margarine, melted
    1 large egg
  3/4 cup finely chopped apple (I leave the skin on for
      flavor, you can peel them if you like)
1 1/2 tablespoons melted butter
  1/2 teaspoon cinnamon

Preheat oven to 400 degrees. In a large bowl, combine the cereal, flour, sugar, baking soda and salt. Mix well with a fork, make a well in the center and set aside. Whisk together in a small bowl the buttermilk, 1/4 cup of melted butter and egg. Stir liquid mixture into center of dry ingredients and fold together until just blended, do not overmix. Let the mixture stand 15 minutes at room temperature. In a separate small bowl, combine the apple, 1 1/2 tablespoons of melted butter and cinnamon. Spoon 1 tablespoon of batter into each of 12* greased muffin tins, or use liners. Cover with a teaspoon of apple mixture for each muffin. Top with remaining batter. Don't be discouraged if some of the apples get mixed up with the batter - I found it easiest to use my fingers to spread the batter evenly! Bake for 20 minutes, or until golden on top and a toothpick inserted into the center of a muffin comes out clean. Cool on a rack slightly before indulging!

MAKES 9-12 MUFFINS

*NOTE: I prefer to make 9 extra-large muffins. If you choose to make 9, put a little water in the three empty muffin tins before baking.

BLUEBERRY - BRAN MUFFINS

20 minutes to prepare   *15-20 minutes to bake*

In an age when getting enough fiber in your diet is of utmost importance, it's nice to find a recipe that includes both bran and taste! These distinctive muffins are so moist and tasty that you almost forget they're good for you. Remember: always wrap homemade muffins tightly in plastic wrap; they get hard and stale very quickly. If they do get stale, place in the microwave with a cup of water and microwave on high for 20-30 seconds—they get moist and chewy again!

2	cups whole wheat flour	2	packed tablespoons brown sugar
1 1/2	cups whole bran	2	cups plain yogurt
3/4	teaspoon salt	1	egg
1 1/4	teaspoon baking soda	1/2	cup honey
1	teaspoon baking powder	2	tablespoons butter or margarine, melted
1	teaspoon fresh lemon rind	1 1/2	cups blueberries (fresh or frozen)*

Preheat oven to 425 degrees. In large bowl, combine the whole wheat flour, bran, salt, baking soda, baking powder, lemon rind and sugar. Mix with a fork until well blended and set aside. In a large mixing bowl, beat together the yogurt, egg, honey and butter. Fold in dry ingredients until just blended (do not overmix or muffins will rubbery). Gently fold in the blueberries. Pour batter into greased muffin tins (or use liners) until 2/3 full. For extra large muffins, fill each tin to the top! Bake for 15-20 minutes or until a toothpick comes out clean. Remove from pan and cool on racks before serving.

MAKES ABOUT 12 MEDIUM SIZE MUFFINS OR 8-10 LARGE

*When using frozen blueberries, keep in freezer until ready to use.

PRESERVE MUFFINS

30-35 minutes to prepare   *18-20 minutes to bake*

What do I mean by preserve? Whatever you want. Create these marvelous muffins with your favorite preserve, raspberry, strawberry, apricot, orange marmalade, etc. Whatever preserve you choose, these muffins are uniquely divine and make a perfect treat to bring along when you've been invited somewhere for the weekend.

1 3/4	cups all-purpose flour
3	teaspoons baking powder
1/2	teaspoon baking soda
1/2	teaspoon salt
2	tablespoons granulated sugar
2	packed tablespoons brown sugar
1	egg
1	cup milk
4	tablespoons butter or margarine, melted
1	tablespoon fresh lemon rind, grated
1/4	cup + 2 tablespoons preserves

Preheat oven to 400 degrees. In a large bowl, sift together the flour, baking powder, baking soda and salt. Add the sugars and gently combine with a fork, to break up the brown sugar. In a separate bowl, beat egg with a wire whisk and add the milk. Blend in the butter, lemon rind and preserves. Mix well with a wire whisk until preserves are in tiny lumps. Make a well in the center of the flour mixture and pour the liquid mixture into the center. Stir with a wooden spoon until just combined (mixture should be lumpy, do NOT overmix or muffins will be rubbery). Pour batter into lightly greased muffin tins, or use liners, until 2/3 full. Bake for 18-20 minutes, or until a toothpick comes out clean. Remove muffins from pan and cool on rack. Taste best when served warm.

MAKES ABOUT 1 DOZEN MUFFINS

GINGER GEMS

25 minutes to prepare   *2 hours to chill*   *10 minutes to bake*

These glorified ginger snaps are a tasty treat created especially for cool fall weekends. Served with apple cider or hot tea, they add a perfect "snap" to your day.

Cookie Dough:

2 1/4 **cups all-purpose flour**
1 1/2 **teaspoons baking soda**
   1 **teaspoon cinnamon**
 1/2 **teaspoon ground cloves**
 1/2 **teaspoon nutmeg**
   1 **teaspoon ground ginger**
 3/4 **cup (1 1/2 sticks) butter or margarine**
   1 **egg**
 1/4 **cup molasses**
   1 **packed cup light brown sugar**

If you were lucky enough to receive a food processor for a wedding gift, these ginger gems are a breeze. If not, they are still easy! Just use a mixer instead.

Combine the flour, baking soda, cinnamon, cloves, nutmeg and ginger in a food processor fitted with the metal blade. Process until well blended. Set aside in separate bowl. Process butter until creamy. Add egg, molasses and sugar and mix well. Gradually add flour mixture and mix until flour is absorbed (do not over-process or the result will be tough, dry cookies). Wrap in plastic wrap and chill for two hours. Preheat oven to 350 degrees. Roll dough into 1" round balls and place on a lightly greased baking sheet. Bake for 10 minutes or until done - cookies should be firm but not hard because they will harden as they cool.

Icing (optional):

> 3   tablespoons butter
> 2   cups confectioners sugar
> 1   teaspoon vanilla extract
> 1   tablespoon milk

In a mixer or food processor combine butter and half of the sugar and process until creamy (it may seem like it won't ever get creamy, but it will!). Add the remaining sugar, vanilla and milk and process until creamy and smooth. If mixture is too dry, add more milk, if it is too runny, add more confectioners sugar. Spread on warm cookies.

MAKES ABOUT 2 DOZEN COOKIES

MARGE'S MOLASSES COOKIES

10-15 minutes to prepare   *1 hour to chill (optional)*   *10-12 minutes to bake*

My mother-in-law is notorious for her molasses cookies. She bakes the best and now you can too! (This makes a large batch of cookies so be prepared to give some away.)

1	cup margarine
1/3	cup Crisco
1/2	cup granulated sugar
1/2	packed cup dark brown sugar
1	teaspoon ground cinnamon
1	teaspoon ground ginger
1	teaspoon salt
5	teaspoons baking soda
1	cup warm water
2	cups dark molasses
5-6	cups all-purpose flour

Beat until creamy the margarine, Crisco and two sugars with a mixer or food processor fitted with the metal blade. Beat in cinnamon, ginger and salt. Dissolve baking soda in warm water. Beat molasses into butter mixture. Beat in 2 1/2 cups of the flour and then water mixture. Add 2 1/2 more cups of flour. Mix well, and add more flour as necessary to form a manageable dough. Cover with plastic wrap and refrigerate for 1 hour (you may choose to skip this part and bake cookies right away). Preheat oven to 350 degrees. Roll dough out about 1/2" thick. Cut out cookies with a cookie cutter (or an upside down glass) and place on lightly greased baking sheets. Bake 10 minutes for soft cookies or 12 minutes for slightly firmer cookies. Cool on wire racks.

MAKES ABOUT 50-60 3" COOKIES

DOLLIE'S FAMOUS CHOCOLATE CHUNK COOKIES

20-25 minutes to prepare   *12 minutes to bake*

My mother is known for her chocolate chunk cookies. It would be a crime if I didn't bless everyone with her recipe. I must warn you, however, that they are addictive, and even the most serious of dieters can't resist. In addition, this recipe is a large one, so plan on bringing some into work, to your neighbor's, etc.

3	cups all-purpose flour
1 1/2	cups oat flour
1 lb.	sweet butter (4 sticks)
2	teaspoons salt
2	teaspoons vanilla extract
1 1/2	cups granulated sugar
1 1/2	packed cups dark brown sugar
4	large eggs
2	teaspoons baking soda
2	teaspoons hot water
3	10 oz. bags chocolate chunks
2-3	10 oz. bags chopped walnuts or pecans (optional)
1/2	cup chopped white chocolate chunks (optional)

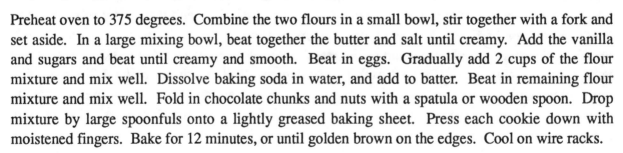

Preheat oven to 375 degrees. Combine the two flours in a small bowl, stir together with a fork and set aside. In a large mixing bowl, beat together the butter and salt until creamy. Add the vanilla and sugars and beat until creamy and smooth. Beat in eggs. Gradually add 2 cups of the flour mixture and mix well. Dissolve baking soda in water, and add to batter. Beat in remaining flour mixture and mix well. Fold in chocolate chunks and nuts with a spatula or wooden spoon. Drop mixture by large spoonfuls onto a lightly greased baking sheet. Press each cookie down with moistened fingers. Bake for 12 minutes, or until golden brown on the edges. Cool on wire racks.

MAKES ABOUT 4-5 DOZEN LARGE COOKIES

OATMEAL/PEANUT BUTTER COOKIES

15-20 minutes to prepare   *10-12 minutes to bake*

These chewy morsels are positively perfect. They are easy to prepare, so make them next time you're looking for something wonderfully different.

3/4	cup (1 1/2 sticks) butter or margarine
3/4	cup peanut butter
1	cup granulated sugar
1	packed cup light brown sugar
2	eggs
1/4	cup milk
1	teaspoon vanilla extract
2	cups all-purpose flour
1	teaspoon baking soda
1/2	teaspoon salt
1/4	teaspoon cinnamon
2	cups rolled oats (not instant)

Preheat oven to 350 degrees. In a mixer, cream together the butter, peanut butter and two sugars. Add the eggs one at a time, mixing well after each addition. Add all remaining ingredients, except for the oatmeal and beat until creamy. Fold in oatmeal and mix well. Drop by rounded teaspoonfuls onto ungreased baking sheets, approximately 1" apart. Bake for 10-12 minutes. When finished, cookies will appear slightly browned and puffy, they flatten as they cool. Cool on rack before serving, or stacking.

MAKES ABOUT 3 DOZEN COOKIES (2 dozen if you make your cookies larger!)

HINT: To add a little spunk to your cookies, add 1 cup of peanuts for a nutty crunch!

APPLE COOKIES

15-20 minutes to prepare   *10-12 minutes to bake*

A perfect treat for the fall blues. In the fall, apples are at their peak. I have taken advantage of that fact and created cookies for all those delectable apples—because they let the apple taste come through and speak for itself.

1/2	cup (1 stick) butter or margarine
1	packed cup light brown sugar
1	egg
1	teaspoon salt
1	teaspoon cinnamon
1/4	teaspoon nutmeg
1/8	teaspoon ground cloves
2	cups all-purpose flour
1	teaspoon baking soda
1/4	cup milk
2	cups tart, fresh apples, chopped

Preheat oven to 400 degrees. In a large mixing bowl, combine the butter and sugar and beat until creamy. Beat in egg. Add salt, cinnamon, nutmeg and cloves and mix well. Add flour, baking soda and milk and stir with a wooden spoon until blended. Fold in apples. Drop by teaspoonfuls onto ungreased baking sheets. Bake for 10-12 minutes or until cookies are firm to the touch. Cool on rack before serving or stacking.

MAKES ABOUT 3 DOZEN COOKIES

BUTTER COOKIES

15-20 minutes to prepare *2 hours to chill* *10-12 minutes to bake*

This basic recipe is all you need to begin a future of great cookie making. Try topping these crispy, buttery, melt-in-your-mouth cookies with colored sprinkles or cinnamon and sugar, or dipping them into melted chocolate and then into crushed nuts, for a fabulous variation.

1/2 **cup (1 stick) butter**
1/2 **cup granulated sugar**
1 **egg**
1/2 **teaspoon vanilla extract**
1/4 **teaspoon lemon or orange rind**
1/4 **teaspoon salt**
1 1/4 **cups all-purpose flour**

In a large mixing bowl or food processor fitted with the metal blade, beat together the butter and sugar until creamy. Add egg, vanilla, lemon rind and salt and mix well. Gradually add flour and mix until a manageable dough forms. Wrap dough in plastic wrap and chill for at least 2 hours.

Preheat oven to 375 degrees. Roll dough out onto a lightly floured surface about 1/4" thick. Cut out shapes with cookie cutters and place on lightly greased baking sheets. Bake for 10-12 minutes, or until edges are golden.

NOTE: If you are going to use sprinkles, lightly brush the top of each cookie with egg white and then top with sprinkles; this will keep the sprinkles from falling off.

MAKES ABOUT 25-30 COOKIES

CINNAMON COOKIES

15 minutes to prepare   *10-12 minutes to bake*

These cookies are a perfect treat for the holidays. Bring them along to holiday parties, or serve them at your own festive affair. This recipe can easily be doubled, if necessary.

          1   **cup all-purpose flour**
          2   **teaspoons ground cinnamon**
        1/4   **cup (1/2 stick) butter, softened**
        1/2   **cup granulated sugar, plus extra to sprinkle on top**
          1   **egg**
          1   **teaspoon vanilla**
        1/4   **cup milk**

Preheat oven to 375 degrees. Sift flour and cinnamon together into a small bowl and set aside. In a large mixing bowl, beat together the butter and sugar until creamy. Beat in egg and vanilla. Gradually add flour mixture and milk, alternating a little of each at a time, ending with flour. Mix until smooth.   Drop by rounded teaspoons onto a lightly greased baking sheet and bake for 10-12 minutes, or until edges are golden. Remove from oven, sprinkle the top of each cookie with granulated sugar and turn to wire racks to cool.

MAKES ABOUT 18-20 COOKIES

BEGINNER'S BROWNIES

15-20 minutes to prepare   *30 minutes to bake*

These scrumptious little morsels are a cinch to make and taste like heaven. It's a basic brownie recipe, one in which many variations can be made. You can add nuts, chocolate chips, mini-marshmallows, fresh orange rind and any other favorite to enhance the flavor of an already incredible chocolatey treat!

- 2 oz. unsweetened chocolate (two 1 oz. squares)
- 2/3 cup all-purpose flour
- 1/2 teaspoon baking powder
- 1/4 teaspoon salt
- 2 eggs
- 1 cup granulated sugar
- 1/4 cup (1/2 stick) butter or margarine, melted
- 1 teaspoon vanilla extract

Melt chocolate in the top of a double boiler or in a small sauce pan set in a larger pan of simmering water. Remove from heat and set aside. Sift together the flour, salt and baking powder. In a large mixing bowl, beat together eggs and sugar. Add butter and mix until blended. Gradually add chocolate to egg mixture and mix well. Beat in vanilla. Gradually add flour mixture and mix well. Pour batter into a lightly greased 8" or 9" baking pan and bake for 30 minutes, or until a toothpick comes out virtually clean. Cool slightly before cutting.

MAKES ABOUT 10 4" BROWNIES

CAROLINE'S FUDGE

5-10 minutes to prepare   *1 hour to chill*

Mouth-watering morsels that will leave you breathless.

18 oz.   chocolate chips
1   can sweetened condensed milk
1   teaspoon vanilla extract
1   tablespoon brandy or rum OR 1 teaspoon fresh orange rind
1   cup chopped nuts, optional

Line the bottom of a shallow baking dish with wax paper and set aside. Melt chocolate chips in a double boiler, or a small sauce pan set inside a larger sauce pan of simmering water, or in the microwave. While chocolate is still hot, stir in sweetened condensed milk, vanilla and liquor or orange rind. Blend until creamy and smooth. Stir in nuts, if desired. Pour mixture into baking dish and refrigerate until firm, about 1 hour minimum. Cut into 2" squares and serve.

MAKES ABOUT 18-20 2" SQUARES

10

Special Occasions

NEW YEAR'S

"Should old acquaintance be forgot..?" Not if you prepare this perfectly delicious dinner delight! It's a must to ring in the new year!

Confetti Salad with Streamers
15-20 minutes to prepare

1 1/2 cups Orzo pasta (pasta shaped like rice)	1 medium tomato, chopped
3 tablespoons red wine vinegar	1 green bell pepper, chopped
1 teaspoon Dijon mustard	1 cucumber, chopped
1 teaspoon olive oil	1 small red onion, chopped
1 carrot, grated in long strips (like streamers)	1/8 cup fresh basil, minced

Cook Orzo according to package directions, drain, rinse under cold water and set aside. In a small bowl, combine the vinegar, mustard and olive oil. Mix well with a wire whisk and set aside. In a large bowl, combine the cooked Orzo, tomato, green pepper, cucumber, onion and basil. Add vinegar mixture and stir gently until all vegetables are coated. Serve on top of Romaine or red lettuce. Garnish the top and sides with grated carrot "streamers" and serve.

Chicken and Mushrooms in Champagne
20-25 minutes to prepare   *40-50 minutes to cook*

(NOTE: I serve this dish with white or brown, fluffy rice on the side to soak up the leftover, delicious cream sauce.)

1 whole chicken breast, halved	6-8 black peppercorns
10-12 fresh mushrooms, sliced	1 teaspoon dried tarragon
1 tablespoon butter or margarine	1/4 teaspoon dried mustard
2 cups dry Champagne	1/2 cup heavy cream

In a large skillet, saute mushrooms in butter until tender. Add chicken breast and saute until golden brown on both sides. Add 1 1/2 cups of Champagne, peppercorns and tarragon. Bring to a boil, reduce heat and simmer, covered, until chicken is tender and cooked through, about 40 minutes. Remove chicken, mushrooms and peppercorns with a slotted spoon. Discard peppercorns and set aside chicken and mushrooms, keep warm. Add remaining champagne and mustard to skillet and reduce liquid by half. Stir in heavy cream and simmer, stirring constantly, until mixture reduces and thickens to a gravy-like consistency. Pour sauce over chicken and serve.

Deluxe Green Beans
20-25 minutes preparation and cooking time

1/2	lb. fresh green beans, or 1 package frozen green beans, thawed and drained		
1	tablespoon butter or margarine	1	tablespoon sour cream
2	tablespoons chopped onion	1/2	teaspoon paprika
1	tablespoon all-purpose flour	1/2	teaspoon salt
1/2	cup beef broth	1/4	teaspoon black pepper
1	tablespoon fresh parsley, chopped		

When using fresh green beans, trim ends, slice in half lengthwise and set aside. Heat butter in a large skillet and add onion. Saute over medium heat until tender. Stir in flour and mix until onion is coated. Stir in beef broth. Add green beans, cover and simmer until beans are tender crisp and sauce has thickened, about 5-7 minutes, stirring frequently. Stir in parsley, sour cream, paprika, salt and pepper. Mix well and simmer until heated through. Serve.

Pecan Pie

20-25 minutes to prepare   *50 minutes to bake*

3	eggs, slightly beaten	1	teaspoon vanilla extract
1/2	cup granulated sugar	1 1/2	cup pecans, broken or chopped
1/2	packed cup brown sugar	12-14	whole pecan halves
3/4	cup light corn syrup	3	tablespoons butter, melted
1	9" uncooked pie shell (recipe follows or a premade one may be substituted)		

Preheat oven to 400 degrees. Press the uncooked pie shell into the bottom of a 9" pie pan, pinch around rim of the plate and set aside. In a large mixing bowl, combine all ingredients but the pecan halves and mix well. Pour filling into pie shell. Arrange the additional pecan halves around the inside edge. Bake for 10 minutes at 400 degrees. Reduce heat to 350 degrees and bake for an additional 40 minutes, or until center and top are firm to the touch (the pie will harden as is cools). Cool on rack before cutting.

Pie Crust:

1 1/2	cups all-purpose flour
1/2	teaspoon salt
1/2	cup (1 stick) butter, cut into chunks
3	tablespoons cold water

In a large bowl or food processor, combine flour, salt and butter. Cut butter into flour with two knives or process until butter is pea-size and mixture resembles coarse meal. Add water, one tablespoon at a time, and mix with a fork or process until a manageable dough forms. Turn to a lightly floured surface (or place between two pieces of wax paper) and roll out to the width of an upside down pie plate. Use as instructed.

VALENTINE'S DAY

For the most romantic night of the year, try the following suggestions for dinner at home. Served with a bottle of wine, candlelight and soft music, this meal can be the start of a beautiful evening.

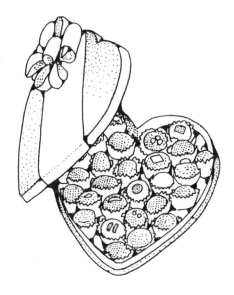

Broiled Petite Lobster Tails

5 minutes to prepare   *2-3 hours to marinate*
10-12 minutes to broil

4-5   petite lobster tails
1/4   cup lemon juice
1/4   cup olive or vegetable oil
1   teaspoon salt
1   teaspoon paprika
1/4   cup green onion, minced
        Water

In a bowl large enough to hold all tails, combine lemon juice, oil, salt, paprika and onion. Add lobster tails and pour in enough water to cover (tails should be immersed in marinade). Cover with plastic wrap and refrigerate for at least 2-3 hours. Remove tails from marinade and with a pair of scissors cut away the thin under-tissue, exposing the meat. Slightly crack the hard shell enabling the tail to lie flat (if you don't do this, the tails will curl up during cooking). Brush a small amount of the marinade on the meat and place 4" under broiler. Broil for 5 minutes on each side, basting frequently with marinade. Serve with melted butter and lemon slices on the side.

Asparagus with Hollandaise
10 minutes to prepare

NOTE: Make the hollandaise just before serving because once prepared, it must be served immediately.

12 asparagus stalks	1/4 teaspoon paprika
4 egg yolks	Dash of black pepper
1/2 teaspoon salt	1 cup butter, melted and
2 tablespoons lemon juice	still hot

Wash asparagus and cut off the coarse ends. Simmer in enough water to cover in a medium size sauce pan or in the microwave until tender crisp, about 5-7 minutes. Drain and set aside (cover to keep warm). In a blender or food processor, combine all remaining ingredients but the butter and mix well. While machine is running, gradually add the hot butter. Process until mixture thickens (should not be longer than 30-60 seconds). Serve in dollops on top of asparagus.

Lemon Rice
25-30 minutes preparation and cooking time

1-2 tablespoons butter or margarine	2 tablespoons lemon juice
2 tablespoons green onion, chopped	1/4 teaspoon black pepper
1 cup uncooked white rice	3 tablespoons fresh parsley, chopped
2 cups chicken broth	

In a medium sauce pan, melt butter over medium high heat. Add onion and saute until tender, about 3-5 minutes. Stir in rice and saute until golden. Add chicken broth, lemon juice and pepper. Bring to a boil over high heat. Cover, reduce heat and simmer until all liquid is absorbed, about 20 minutes.   Just before serving, toss in parsley and mix well with a fork.

Heart-Shaped Strawberry Shortcake

20-25 minutes to prepare   *20 minutes to bake*

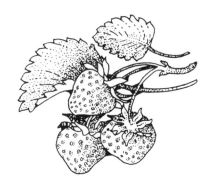

1   **pint fresh strawberries**
1   **tablespoon orange juice**
3   **tablespoons granulated sugar**
1   **cup all-purpose flour**
2   **teaspoons baking powder**
     Pinch of salt
2   **tablespoons butter**
1/4 **cup plus 2 tablespoons milk**
     Whipped cream for topping

Core strawberries and place all but two in a food processor or blender. Add orange juice and 1 tablespoon of the sugar and process until strawberries are in small chunks and mixture is blended. Pour mixture into a small bowl and set aside. Preheat oven to 400 degrees. Sift flour, remaining sugar, baking powder and salt into a large bowl or food processor fitted with the metal blade. Work butter into flour mixture with two knives or process until mixture resembles coarse meal. Gradually add milk and work in with a fork or process until a manageable dough forms. Turn to a lightly floured surface and roll dough out about 3/4" thick. Cut into 2 large heart shapes* (about 4" wide). If you have remaining dough, roll it into a ball or make an extra heart. Place on a lightly greased baking sheet and bake for 20 minutes, or until golden. Remove from oven and while still warm, use a fork to split cakes in half (like an English muffin).

To assemble: Spoon 1/2 of the strawberry mixture on bottom halves of both cakes. Top with second half of cake and then remaining strawberry mixture. Top with whipped cream. Slice remaining two strawberries and stick into whipped cream as garnish. Serve with love.

*Note: If you don't have a heart shaped cutter, don't fret - just take a piece of cardboard or thick paper and draw a heart. Cut out the heart and use it as a guide while you cut the dough with a sharp knife.

THANKSGIVING

For many people, Thanksgiving is a day to spend with family. People will drive all day just to spend this occasion with close relatives. Since Thanksgiving is such a special occasion, and everyone you care about is involved, wouldn't it be nice to invite everyone to your place? (Even if you decide not to entertain at your place, this Thanksgiving feast is perfect for the two of you - with plenty of leftovers!) I suggest making the dessert first, followed by the turkey. While the turkey cooks, prepare the creamed onions and potatoes. When the turkey is finished, put the onions and potatoes in the oven (the onions require about 20 minutes less cooking time than the potatoes). This enables you to carve the turkey and serve everything at once when the vegetables are finished.

Roast Turkey with Stuffing

20-25 minutes to prepare   *2 -4 hours to bake*

- 1 **8-12 lb. turkey**
- 1 **tablespoon butter or margarine**
- 1 **medium onion, chopped**
- 4 **celery stalks, chopped**
- 1 **apple, cored and chopped**
- 1 **teaspoon salt**
- 1/2 **teaspoon black pepper**
- 1 **tablespoon dried parsley**
- 1 **tablespoon oregano**
- 5 **cups dry white bread cubes**
  (or day-old bread chopped into cubes)
- 2 **cups chicken broth**

Preheat oven to 450 degrees. Remove giblets, heart and liver from inside of bird and discard or reserve for another use. Rinse the bird inside and out, pat dry and sprinkle the inside and out with salt and pepper. Set in a large roasting pan and set aside. In a large skillet, melt butter over medium heat. Add onion, celery and apple and saute until tender, about 3-5 minutes. Stir in salt, pepper, parsley and oregano. Remove from heat and pour into a large bowl. Stir in bread cubes and chicken broth and mix well. Stuff mixture loosely into breast cavity of the bird until 2/3 full* (the stuffing will expand during cooking). Return drumsticks to tucked position. If you have one, insert meat thermometer into breast meat. Place turkey in hot oven and immediately reduce temperature to 350 degrees. Bake for 2-4 hours, depending on the size of the bird, basting frequently after the first 30 minutes of roasting. You can usually depend on 20-25 minutes per pound for a stuffed bird and an internal temperature that reaches 190 degrees.

*Note: Stuff the bird JUST before cooking, DO NOT stuff a bird in advance or contamination may occur.

SERVES 4-6

Pan Gravy

10-12	fresh mushrooms, sliced	2/3	cup milk
1	tablespoon butter or margarine	1/3	cup dry sherry
	Roasting pan juices		Salt and black pepper to taste
2	tablespoons all-purpose flour		

Saute mushrooms in butter until tender and set aside. Remove bird from roasting pan and strain remaining juices to remove some of the excess fat. Pour 2 tablespoons of the pan juices into a sauce pan set over medium heat. Add the flour and stir with a wire whisk until smooth. Gradually add remaining pan juices, milk and sherry, stirring constantly with a wire whisk. When mixture thickens, stir in mushrooms. Season with salt and pepper and serve over sliced turkey.

Creamed Onions

10-15 minutes to prepare   *35-40 minutes to bake*

2	tablespoons butter or margarine	1	cup sharp Cheddar cheese, grated
2	tablespoons all-purpose flour	1/4	teaspoon salt
2	cups milk	1/8	teaspoon white pepper
2	14 oz. jars of whole or pearl onions	1/4	cup bread crumbs

Preheat oven to 375 degrees. In a small sauce pan, melt butter over medium heat. Add flour and mix with a wire whisk until mixture is smooth, about 2-3 minutes. Gradually add milk, stirring constantly. When mixture thickens, add onions and mix well. Add cheese, salt and pepper and simmer until cheese melts, stirring constantly. Pour mixture into a 2 quart casserole dish and cover with an even layer of bread crumbs. Bake for 35-40 minutes, until set and bread crumbs are golden brown. Serve hot.

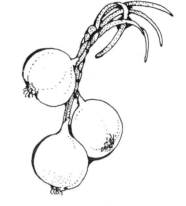

SERVES 4-6

Candied Sweet Potatoes

10-15 minutes to prepare   *1 hour to bake*

4 tablespoons (1/2 stick) butter	3-4 large sweet potatoes or yams
1/4 cup plus 2 tablespoons brown sugar	1/4 cup maple syrup

Preheat oven to 375 degrees. In a small sauce pan combine 2 tablespoons of the butter and 1/4 cup of the brown sugar. Heat over medium heat until both are melted and mixture is smooth, stirring frequently. Pour mixture into the bottom of a shallow baking dish and set aside. Scrub sweet potatoes or yams and slice in half horizontally. Slice each half in half and place side by side on top of butter mixture in baking dish. Combine remaining 2 tablespoons of butter, 2 tablespoons of brown sugar and maple syrup in saucepan. Heat until butter and sugar are melted and mixture is smooth. Pour mixture evenly over sliced potatoes. Cover with foil and bake for 1 hour, or until potatoes are tender. Spoon sweet sauce over potatoes one or two times during cooking. Serve hot.

SERVES 4-6

Pumpkin Pie

10-15 minutes to prepare   *55-60 minutes to bake*

2	eggs
16	oz. canned pumpkin
1/2	cup granulated sugar
1/4	cup packed brown sugar
1/2	teaspoon salt
1 1/4	teaspoons ground cinnamon
1/4	teaspoon ground ginger
1/4	teaspoon ground cloves

1 1/2	cups light cream or evaporated milk
2	tablespoons brandy
1	9" uncooked pie crust (recipe follows or a premade one may be substituted)
	Whipped cream for topping

Preheat oven to 425 degrees. Press uncooked pie shell into the bottom of a 9" pie plate. Pinch the edges with your fingers and set aside. In a large bowl, beat eggs slightly. Add remaining ingredients and mix well with a wire whisk. Pour mixture into pie shell and bake for 15 minutes. Reduce oven temperature to 350 degrees and bake for 40-50 minutes, or until a knife comes out clean. If desired, serve with a dollop of whipped cream on top.

Pie Crust:

1 1/2	cups all-purpose flour
1/2	teaspoon salt

1/2	cup (1 stick) butter or margarine*
3	tablespoons cold water

Sift the flour before measuring and sift again with the salt. Cut the butter into small chunks and add to flour. Cut butter into flour with two knives or a food processor fitted with the metal blade until butter is pea-size and mixture resembles coarse meal. Add water, one tablespoon at a time, and work together with a fork or process until a manageable dough forms. Roll dough into a ball and turn to a lightly floured surface. Roll out with a rolling pin until dough is the size of an upside down 9" pie pan. Press dough firmly into pie pan and trim any excess dough that hangs over the edges. Pie crust is ready to be filled.

*NOTE: Using margarine will make the crust more mealy, rather than flaky in texture.

HOLIDAY DINNER

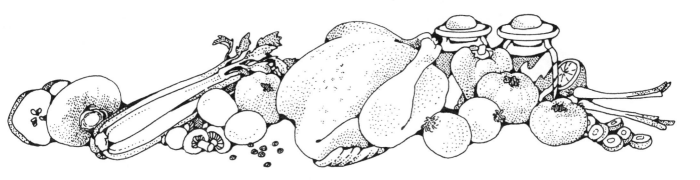

I labeled this "Holiday Dinner" so that whatever holiday you celebrate, this meal will be appropriate. My father cooks once a year, on Christmas. He learned to prepare this meal from Chef Tell, and has perfected it. This dinner is renowned to all family and friends, and it's the perfect meal for holiday celebrations in your home.

Dad's Christmas Goose

10 minutes to prepare   *2 1/2 - 3 hours to bake*

1   **8-10 lb. goose**   1   **apple, cored and sliced**
    Salt and black pepper   1   **medium onion, sliced**
    Thyme (dried)   **Water**

Preheat oven to 425 degrees. Remove any giblets from goose and rinse well, inside and out. Season goose, inside cavity and out, with salt and pepper. Season inside of cavity with a generous amount of thyme. Place breast side down in a large roasting pan. Distribute apple and onion slices evenly around goose. Add enough water to fill the pan about 1". Place goose in hot oven and immediately reduce heat to 350 degrees. Roast for 2 - 2 1/2 hours, basting occasionally. Remove goose from oven and pour off all but 1 cup of liquid. Turn goose over, breast side up and return to oven. Cook until brown, about 20-30 minutes. Remove from oven and place goose on carving board. Deglaze the bottom of the roasting pan by heating over medium heat, adding water and scraping up the brown bits from the bottom of the pan. Reduce liquid in half and add more water. Reduce liquid in half again. Continue cooking until liquid has thickened and has a syrup-like consistency. Strain off any grease and set aside to serve with the carved goose.

SERVES 6-8

Red Cabbage

10 minutes to prepare   *2 hours to cook*

1	head red cabbage	1	cup water
1	medium onion, chopped	1/3	cup granulated sugar
2	apples, cored and thinly sliced	3	tablespoons honey
2	tablespoons butter or margarine	1	teaspoon cinnamon
1/2	cup red wine vinegar	1/2	teaspoon salt
1	cup dry red wine	1/4	teaspoon black pepper
		1	small potato

Peel the outer leaves from the cabbage. Slice cabbage in half and then each half in half. Remove core, shred remaining cabbage with a food processor or sharp knife and set aside. Heat the butter in a large stock pot over medium heat. Stir in onion and apples and saute until tender, about 3-5 minutes. Stir in cabbage, vinegar, wine, 1/2 cup of the water, sugar, honey, cinnamon, salt and pepper. Cover and simmer for 1 hour and 30 minutes, stirring occasionally and adding remaining water as necessary to prevent cabbage from sticking to the bottom of the pan. Peel and grate potato and add to cabbage. Mix well and continue cooking until mixture thickens, about 30 minutes, stirring occasionally. Serve warm.

SERVES 6-8

Spatzle

(Spatzle is a pasta-like dough that can be found in supermarkets or specialty stores.)

15-20 minutes preparation and cooking time

- **2 lbs. spatzle**
- **2-4 tablespoons butter or margarine**
  Salt and black pepper to taste

Cook spatzle according to package directions. Drain and pour into a large skillet with butter. Heat over medium heat until butter is melted and spatzle is moist. Season with salt and pepper and serve.

SERVES 6-8

Chocolate Almond Torte

30-35 minutes to prepare   *40-45 minutes to bake*

- **3/4 cup crushed almonds (if you buy them whole, crush them in a food processor or blender)**
- **1 cup cake flour, sifted after measuring**
- **1 teaspoon baking powder**
- **1/4 teaspoon salt**
- **4 eggs, separated**
- **1 cup granulated sugar**
- **1 teaspoon almond extract**
- **1/4 cup (1/2 stick) butter or margarine, melted**
  Sliced almonds as garnish (optional)

Filling:

- **2 oz. unsweetened chocolate (two 1 oz. squares)**
- **1/2 cup (1 stick) butter**
- **1 egg yolk**
- **1 teaspoon vanilla extract**
- **2 cups confectioners sugar, sifted**

Preheat oven to 325 degrees. Lightly grease an 8" springform pan and sprinkle in 1/4 cup of the crushed almonds. Turn the pan to evenly coat the bottom and sides with almonds. In a large bowl, combine the remaining almonds, flour, baking powder and salt. Mix together with a fork and set aside. In a large mixing bowl, beat egg whites until soft peaks form. While mixer is running, gradually beat in 1/2 cup of the granulated sugar and mix until stiff peaks form. In a separate, small mixing bowl, beat the egg yolks, remaining 1/2 cup of sugar, almond extract and melted butter. Beat until mixture is thick and pale. Fold a large spoonful of egg whites into egg yolk mixture and then fold in the rest. Fold in flour mixture until just blended - do not over-mix. Pour batter into prepared springform pan and bake for 40-45 minutes or until golden brown on top and cake springs back when pressed with your fingers. Cool in pan, on rack thoroughly before removing cake from pan. Split cake in half horizontally with a sharp knife (as if you were cutting an English muffin). Spread buttercream filling (directions follow) evenly on the bottom layer. Place the top layer of cake on top and sift a small amount of confectioners sugar on the surface. Garnish with sliced almonds if desired.

To make the filling:

Melt the chocolate in the top of a double boiler or in a small sauce pan set inside a larger sauce pan of simmering water. Set aside to cool. Beat together butter, egg yolk and vanilla in a mixer or food processor until creamy and smooth. Gradually add confectioners sugar and beat until creamy. While mixer or processor is running, gradually add melted chocolate and blend until light and fluffy. Spread on torte as directed.

MAKES ONE 8" TORTE

ONE YEAR ANNIVERSARY

If you decide to spend your first year anniversary at home, try this romantic and perfectly delicious dinner for two love-birds. I have not given you a special dessert, since we all know what you will be pulling out of the freezer!

Caesar Salad

20-30 minutes to prepare

6	leaves Romaine lettuce
4	slices of french bread, sliced 1/2" thick
2	tablespoons olive or vegetable oil
2	cloves garlic
4-6	anchovy fillets (optional)
1	egg
2	tablespoons fresh lemon juice
1	tablespoon red wine vinegar
1	teaspoon Worcestershire sauce

1/4	teaspoon dry mustard
	Salt and black pepper to taste
1/4	cup grated Parmesan cheese

Wash and dry lettuce leaves and place in refrigerator to crisp. Preheat oven to 400 degrees. Place bread slices on an ungreased baking sheet and bake until crisp, about 8-10 minutes. Remove bread from oven, brush slices with oil and return to oven for 15 minutes, or until brown. In a small bowl, crush together the garlic and anchovies, reserving 2 anchovies as garnish if desired. Gradually add 1 tablespoon of oil and mix well. Spread this mixture on the bread slices and cut slices into small cubes, set aside. Bring a small pot of water to a boil and add the egg (in shell). Boil egg for 1 minute and remove from pan. Remove lettuce from refrigerator and tear into bite size pieces. In a large bowl, combine the lettuce, egg, bread cubes, remaining oil, lemon juice, vinegar, Worcestershire sauce, Parmesan cheese and dry mustard. Toss until combined and season with salt and freshly ground black pepper. Serve with anchovy fillets on top.

Cornish Hens with Sweet Rice Stuffing
1 1/2 -2 hours preparation and cooking time

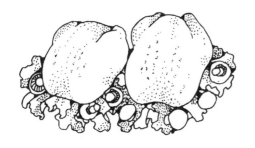

2	Cornish hens, about 1 - 1 1/2 lbs. each
	Salt and ground black pepper
1/2	cup grapes
1/3	cup brandy or Cognac
2/3	cup white rice
1	tablespoon minced onion
1	stalk celery, chopped
1	tablespoon butter or margarine
1/4	teaspoon salt
1/4	teaspoon pepper

Baste with:

1/4 cup honey   1 tablespoon Dijon mustard

Cook rice according to package directions and set aside. Preheat oven to 450 degrees. Remove giblets from inside of hens and discard or reserve for another use. Rinse hens thoroughly inside and out and pat dry. Season each hen lightly with salt and pepper inside and out, set aside. Simmer grapes in brandy for 15 minutes, remove from heat and set aside. Melt butter in a large skillet over medium heat. Add onion and celery and saute until tender, about 3-5 minutes. Stir in cooked rice, grapes, salt and pepper. Mix well with a fork. Spoon stuffing loosely into the cavity of the hens (reserve any leftover stuffing as a side dish). Place hens in roasting pan and place in oven. Immediately reduce heat to 350 degrees and bake for 1 hour and 15 minutes, or until tender (hens are finished when juices run clear when thigh is pierced at its thickest point). In a small saucepan, combine the honey and mustard. Heat over low heat while stirring with a wire whisk. Baste hens with honey mixture after the first 30 minutes of cooking (every 15 minutes or so thereafter).

Corn with Red Peppers

10 minutes to prepare

1 **package frozen sweet corn**
1 **medium sweet red pepper, chopped**
1 **tablespoon butter or margarine**
Salt and ground black pepper to taste

In a large skillet, melt the butter over medium heat. Add corn and red pepper and saute until corn is heated through and pepper is tender crisp. Season with salt and pepper and serve.

SUNDAY BRUNCH

Sunday brunch is sometimes more fun than an evening party. The following recipes provide you with several different ideas on what to serve when you invite guests over for a Sunday of fun. Select one, some or all of the dishes below and expect your guests to come back for seconds!

Country Style Ham and Eggs

20-25 minutes to prepare

25-30 minutes to bake

2 medium potatoes
1 tablespoon butter or margarine
1 small onion, thinly sliced
1/4 lb. ham, sliced 1/8" thick and cut into 1" squares
10 eggs
1 tablespoon Dijon mustard
1/4 cup fresh parsley, chopped
1/2 packed cup grated Cheddar or Swiss cheese
Paprika

Use a cast iron skillet or 2 quart casserole dish for this recipe. Boil potatoes in enough lightly salted water to cover until tender, about 15-20 minutes (or until they fall off a fork when pricked). Drain and set aside. Preheat oven to 400 degrees. In a large mixing bowl, beat eggs with a wire whisk. Add parsley and mustard, mix well and set aside. Place butter in skillet or casserole and place in oven to melt. Remove dish from oven and cover bottom with an even layer of onion slices. Return dish to oven and bake until onions are golden, about 5-7 minutes. Remove skillet from oven and reduce temperature to 350 degrees. Slice potatoes in half and then into thin slices. Spread ham on top of onions, followed by the potato slices. Pour egg mixture over everything and sprinkle the top with grated cheese. Sprinkle the top with paprika and bake for 25-30 minutes, or until eggs are set and casserole is golden brown. Serve warm or cold.

SERVES 4-6

Broccoli and Cheese Quiche

25-30 minutes to prepare   *30 minutes to bake*

- 2 **cups fresh broccoli florets**
- 1 **tablespoon butter or margarine**
- 2 **tablespoons minced onion**
- 1/2 **cup Ricotta cheese**
- 1/2 **cup cottage cheese**
- 1/4 **packed cup grated Swiss cheese**
- 1 **tablespoon Dijon mustard**
- 1/2 **teaspoon salt**
- 1/4 **teaspoon ground black pepper**
- 1/4 **teaspoon paprika**
- 2 **eggs, lightly beaten**
- 1/2 **cup heavy cream**
- 2 **tablespoons grated Cheddar cheese (optional)**
- 1 **9" uncooked pie shell (recipe follows or a premade one may be substituted)**

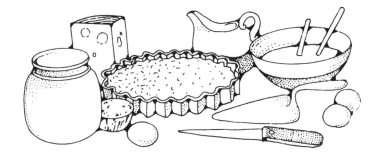

Preheat oven to 375 degrees. Press uncooked pie shell into the bottom of a 9" pie plate and pinch down the edges. Pierce the shell several times with a fork and set aside. Blanche broccoli in a large pot of rapidly boiling water for 1 minute. Drain and set aside. In a large skillet, saute onion in butter until tender, about 3-5 minutes. Stir in Ricotta, cottage and Swiss cheeses. Add mustard, salt, pepper and paprika and mix well. Add eggs and cream and mix well. Chop broccoli into small pieces and fold into cheese mixture. Pour mixture into pie shell and sprinkle the top with grated Cheddar cheese, if desired. Bake for 30 minutes or until set. Cool slightly before serving.

SERVES 6-8

Pie Crust:

1 1/2 cups all-purpose flour	1/2 cup (1 stick) butter, cold
1/2 teaspoon salt	3 tablespoons cold water

Sift the flour before measuring and sift again with the salt. Cut the butter into small chunks and add to the flour. Work butter into flour with two knives or a food processor fitted with the metal blade until butter is pea-size and mixture resembles coarse meal. Add water, one tablespoon at a time, and blend together or process until a manageable dough forms. Turn dough to a lightly floured surface (or place between 2 pieces of wax paper) and roll out until it is 1" larger than your upside down pie plate. Use as instructed in recipe.

Applesauce Coffee Cake

25-30 minutes to prepare   *35-40 minutes to bake*

1/4 cup (1/2 stick) butter	1/2 cup milk
1 cup granulated sugar	1 1/2 cups all-purpose flour
2 eggs, separated	1 teaspoon vanilla extract
2 teaspoons baking powder	1 teaspoon salt
	Confectioners sugar for topping

Filling: (you may substitute premade applesauce from a jar)

8 medium tart apples (i.e., Mackintosh)
1/4 cup granulated sugar
1 teaspoon cinnamon

Preheat oven to 350 degrees. Cream together the butter and sugar. Add egg yolks and mix until creamy. Beat in baking powder, salt, milk, flour and vanilla and blend until smooth. In a small mixing bowl, beat egg whites until stiff. Fold a large spoonful of egg whites into batter and then fold in the rest. Mix well. Pour batter into a lightly greased, 9" cake pan and bake for 35-40 minutes, or until a knife comes out clean. Cool on wire rack.

To make the filling: Boil apples in a large pot of water until tender, about 8-10 minutes. Drain and smash through a strainer or fine sieve into a large bowl. To the pulp, add the sugar and cinnamon (adjusting the amounts to suit your taste).

After cake has cooled on a rack for at least 30 minutes, carefully take a sharp knife and cut the cake in half horizontally. Remove the top piece and set aside. Pour an even layer of apple sauce on the bottom layer. Cover with the second layer of cake. Sift confectioners sugar on top of cake and serve.

MAKES ONE 9" CAKE

Sticky Buns

35-45 minutes to prepare   *1 1/2 hours to rise*   *18-20 minutes to bake*

My mother discovered this recipe from her camp counselor when she was a kid. She modified it, however, since he made enough to serve hundreds of kids! These sticky buns can be made ahead and frozen until ready to eat. Reheat in a 300 degree oven for 20-30 minutes.

1/4	packed cup light brown sugar	2	eggs, beaten slightly
2	tablespoons butter, melted	3	tablespoons butter, melted
1/4	cup maple syrup	1/2	teaspoon salt
1	cup warm milk (warm in microwave for 1 minute on 50%)	3 1/2 - 4	cups all-purpose flour, sifted before measuring
1	packet dry active yeast		Raisins
1/4	cup granulated sugar		Walnuts or pecans, crushed or broken into little pieces

Filling:

1/3	packed cup light brown sugar	1	tablespoon cinnamon
2	tablespoons butter, melted	1/4	cup maple syrup

In a small bowl, combine the brown sugar, 2 tablespoons of melted butter and maple syrup. Pour mixture evenly into two 9" cake pans and cover with a generous amount of raisins and crushed nuts, set aside. Dissolve yeast in warm milk, add sugar and set aside. In a large bowl, combine eggs, 3 tablespoons of melted butter and salt. Add milk mixture and mix well with a wire whisk. Add flour and mix together with a wooden spoon. Turn to a lightly floured surface and knead for 10 minutes, adding more flour if necessary to prevent dough from sticking (if you have a mixer equipped with a dough hook, mix for 2 minutes and knead on the appropriate speed for 2-3 minutes, or until a manageable dough has formed and is no longer sticking to the sides of the bowl). Place dough in a lightly oiled bowl and turn to coat all sides. Cover with a damp cloth or dish towel and let rise in a warm place, free from draft, until doubled in bulk, about 1 hour. Punch down dough with your fist and let sit for 15 minutes. While you wait, combine the filling ingredients in a small bowl and mix well with a wire whisk. Turn dough out onto a lightly floured surface and roll out a large rectangle, about 1/4" thick. Pour the filling on top and spread it into an even layer using a spatula or the back of a spoon. Top with a generous amount of raisins and crushed nuts. Roll up tightly from the smaller end in a jellyroll fashion. Slice roll into 1 1/2" slices and place 1/2" apart in prepared cake pans (if cutting the dough has crushed it, reshape into a circle with your hands). Cover with wax paper and let rise until doubled in bulk, about 30 minutes. Preheat oven to 375 degrees. Remove wax paper and bake sticky buns for 18-20 minutes, or until golden brown on top. Remove from oven, let stand at room temperature for 1 minute, and invert onto serving plates. Serve warm if possible.

MAKES 14-16 STICKY BUNS

Rolled Cinnamon Bread

25-30 minutes to prepare　　　*1 hour and 45 minutes to rise*　　　*40 minutes to bake*

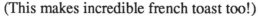

(This makes incredible french toast too!)

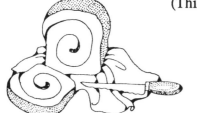

1/2　cup buttermilk	2　cups all-purpose flour
1　packet dry active yeast	2　eggs
1/8　cup granulated sugar	1　tablespoon honey
2　tablespoons butter, melted	1　tablespoon water
1/2　teaspoon salt	

Filling:

1/4 cup granulated sugar	1 1/2 teaspoons cinnamon

In a small sauce pan or in the microwave, heat the buttermilk to lukewarm. Sprinkle the yeast into the buttermilk and set aside to dissolve. In a separate bowl, combine the sugar, melted butter and salt, set aside. Add the buttermilk mixture to one cup of the flour and mix well with a wooden spoon. Blend in the sugar mixture. Add 1 egg, honey and remaining flour and mix well. Knead dough with a mixer equipped with a dough hook for 2 minutes or turn dough to a lightly floured surface and knead for 10 minutes, until smooth and elastic. Place dough in a lightly oiled bowl and turn to coat all sides. Cover with a dish towel and set in a warm place to rise until doubled in bulk, about 1 hour. Punch down dough with your fist and remove from bowl. Preheat oven to 400 degrees. In a small bowl, combine the remaining egg and tablespoon of water and mix with a wire whisk. In a separate bowl, combine cinnamon and 1/4 cup of sugar and mix with a fork until blended. Roll dough out onto a lightly floured surface in the shape of a rectangle, approximately 8" X 12". Brush the surface with egg, and cover with cinnamon and sugar mixture. Starting from the 8" side, tightly roll up the dough jellyroll fashion. Place in a lightly greased bread pan, brush the surface with egg, cover with a dish towel and set in a warm place to rise until doubled in bulk, about 45 minutes. Bake for 15 minutes at 400 degrees. Reduce heat to 350 degrees and bake for an additional 25 minutes. Cool on rack before serving.

MAKES 1 LOAF

VARIATION: Sprinkle raisins and/or nuts on top of filling mixture before rolling up.

SUPERBOWL SUNDAY

Superbowl Sunday is a great time to invite friends and family over to watch the game. Since the game begins in the late afternoon, you have the morning to put together a sensational meal. The following is a fun feast that can be prepared before your guests arrive, enabling you to enjoy the game—and your guests!

Superbowl Chili

(This recipe is enough for 6-8 people. If you invite more, increase all ingredients accordingly.)

20-25 minutes to prepare   *1-2 hours to cook*

1-2	tablespoons olive or vegetable oil
1	large onion, chopped
4	celery stalks, chopped
3	lbs. ground beef
1/2	cup chili powder
10-12	Italian plum tomatoes, sliced
3	cups beef broth
1	cup tomato sauce
2	teaspoons cumin
1	teaspoon celery seed

2	teaspoons crushed red pepper (more or less to taste)
4	small cans (or 2 large) red kidney beans
	Salt and black pepper to taste
	Cheddar cheese for topping

Heat oil in a large stock pot and add onions and celery. Saute over medium heat until tender, about 3-5 minutes. Add meat and cook until brown, breaking up the meat as it cooks. (If desired, at this point the beef may be drained of fat in a colander and returned to the pot). Add chili powder and stir until all meat is covered. Add all remaining ingredients except for the kidney beans and stir until combined. Simmer over medium-low heat at least 1-2 hours. 30 minutes before serving, add the kidney beans and continue cooking. If liquid is needed during the cooking time, add water or additional tomato sauce, a little at a time. If chili is too watery, crush up some of the kidney beans before adding to the pot, they will absorb some liquid. Serve in bowls with grated cheddar cheese on top.

NOTE: Spices can be varied according to your personal taste.

SERVES 6-8

Cheddar Bread Sticks

This can be made in advance and refrigerated until ready to cook. Recipe can be doubled if necessary.

15-20 minutes to prepare   *30 minutes to bake*

1	cup water
1/4	cup (1/2 stick) butter
1/2	teaspoon salt
1/4	teaspoon pepper
1	cup all-purpose flour
1/4	cup buttermilk
2	eggs
1	cup sharp Cheddar cheese, grated

Preheat oven to 425 degrees. Place water, butter, salt and pepper in a large sauce pan and bring to a boil. When butter is completely melted, add flour and continue cooking, stirring constantly, until mixture becomes thick and leaves the sides of the pan. Remove from heat and beat in buttermilk with a wire whisk. Beat in eggs one at a time, mixing well after each addition. Stir in grated cheese. Form dough into 6" long sticks and place on a lightly greased baking sheet 2 inches apart. Bake for 30 minutes, or until puffy and golden brown. Cool on rack before serving.

MAKES 14-16 BREAD STICKS

Oatmeal Raisin Bars

15-20 minutes to prepare   *35-45 minutes to bake*

2/3   cup all-purpose flour
  1   teaspoon ground cinnamon
1/4   teaspoon salt
1/2   teaspoon baking soda
1/2   cup (1 stick) butter
3/4   packed cup brown sugar
1/2   cup granulated sugar
  1   egg
  1   teaspoon vanilla extract
1/4   cup plus 2 tablespoons milk
  3   cups instant or quick cooking oats
  1   cup raisins

Preheat oven to 350 degrees. Sift together the flour, cinnamon, salt and baking soda, set aside. In a large mixing bowl, beat together the butter and two sugars until creamy. Add egg and mix well. Beat in vanilla and milk. Gradually add flour mixture and mix until smooth. Fold in oats and raisins. Pour mixture into a lightly greased 9" shallow baking dish and bake for 35-45 minutes or until a knife inserted into the center comes out clean (do not over-bake or bars will be dry). Cool slightly before cutting. Cut into 12-16 bars and serve.

MAKES 12-16 BARS

PICNIC BASKET FOR TWO

There is nothing more enjoyable than taking a stroll with your favorite person in an open meadow or along a river bank. This picturesque adventure can be made even more romantic by spreading out a big cozy blanket and picnic basket full of goodies. The following recipes are my suggestions for your basket. You can create your own romantic meal for two, however, I believe there are two staples for every picnic - a bottle of wine and grapes (the most fun is when you peel the grapes for each other!) And don't forget the bottle opener!

Chicken Salad
20-25 minutes to prepare

1 whole boneless chicken breast, skinned	1 teaspoon fresh dill weed or 1/2 teaspoon dried
1/3 cup mayonnaise	2 tablespoons white wine vinegar
1/3 cup plain yogurt	1/4 cup red onion, chopped
2 teaspoons Dijon mustard	1/2 cup pitted black olives, halved
1/2 teaspoon salt	1 celery stalk, chopped
1/2 teaspoon black pepper	1 cup cherry tomatoes, halved

Poach chicken breasts by placing in a large pot with just enough water to cover. Bring water to the simmering stage (not boiling) over low heat. Simmer chicken for 10 minutes, until cooked through. While the chicken is poaching, combine mayonnaise and yogurt. Mix well with a wire whisk. Stir in mustard, salt, pepper, dill and vinegar. Add onion, olives and celery. Remove chicken from pot and cut into bite size chunks. Stir into mayonnaise mixture while still warm. Gently fold in cherry tomatoes. If you have time, cover with plastic wrap and chill to allow the flavors to combine.

Crescent Rolls

20-25 minutes to prepare   *15-30 minutes to rise*   *10-12 minutes to bake*

1	cup milk	3/4 teaspoon salt
1/2	cup water	2 packets dry active yeast
1	tablespoon butter	3 1/2 - 4 1/2 cups all-purpose flour
2	tablespoons granulated sugar	2-3 tablespoons butter, melted

Scald milk in a small sauce pan. Remove from heat and stir in water, 1 tablespoon of butter, sugar and salt. Cool to lukewarm. Sprinkle yeast over milk mixture and set aside for 5 minutes to dissolve. Pour milk mixture into a large mixing bowl or food processor fitted with a metal blade. Add 3 1/2 cups of the flour and work in with a fork or process until a manageable dough forms, adding more flour as necessary to keep dough from sticking to the sides of bowl. Turn to a lightly floured surface and knead until smooth and elastic. Place in a lightly oiled bowl and turn to coat all sides. Cover with a towel, and let rise in a warm place until doubled in bulk, about 15-30 minutes. Preheat oven to 425 degrees. Remove dough from bowl, divide in half and turn to a lightly floured surface. Roll each half into a large circle, about 1/4" thick. Brush the surface with melted butter and cut into 8 wedges each, as you would cut a pie. Roll each wedge from the wider side and place point side down on a lightly greased baking sheet. Bake crescents for 10-12 minutes, or until golden. Cool slightly before serving or wrapping.

MAKES 16 CRESCENT ROLLS

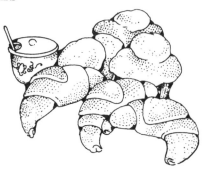

BREAKFAST IN BED

What would a "Newlywed Cookbook" be without Breakfast in Bed?!

Eggs Benedict

(Halve this recipe if you are not planning to eat with your spouse!)

10-20 minutes to prepare

- 4 eggs
- 4 slices canadian bacon, or ham (or 8 slices bacon)
- 2 English muffins, toasted
  Hollandaise - see recipe below

In a medium sauce pan bring 4-6 cups water to a boil. Break each egg into a small bowl or glass (one at a time) before placing in water. Put eggs in water, one at a time, and simmer for 5 minutes, never letting the water reach the boiling point again.

In a large skillet cook the bacon or ham until tender crisp. Remove from skillet and place on paper towels to drain. Place bacon on toasted english muffins, top with poached eggs and pour hollandaise on top. Serve immediately.

Hollandaise

- 4 egg yolks
- 1/2 teaspoon salt
- 2 tablespoons lemon juice
- 1/4 teaspoon paprika
  Dash of black pepper
- 1 cup butter, melted and still hot

Combine all ingredients but the butter in a blender or food processor fitted with the metal blade. Process until well blended. While machine is running, gradually add hot butter. Process until mixture thickens, about 30-60 seconds. Serve immediately.

Heavenly Home Fries
20-50* minutes preparation and cooking time

4-5	small new red potatoes, cut into bite size pieces*
1	tablespoon butter or margarine
2	tablespoons chopped onion
1/2	teaspoon paprika
2	tablespoons red wine vinegar
	Salt and black pepper to taste

In a large skillet, melt butter over medium heat. Add onion and saute until tender. Add potatoes, paprika, red wine vinegar, salt and pepper. Saute over medium heat, stirring occasionally, until tender, about 40-45 minutes for raw potatoes.

*To decrease cooking time, parboil the potatoes by immersing whole potatoes into rapidly boiling salt water. Boil until tender, (they will fall off a fork when pricked) about 15-20 minutes. Cool slightly before slicing.

If you have it, garnish the plate with fresh parsley, slices of fresh fruit and of course - a flower!

WHEN INLAWS COME FOR DINNER

Cooking for inlaws can be rather intimidating. You want to impress, however, you don't want to attempt anything that may be too difficult - and flop! The following is a fail-safe dinner for four. Follow the directions and you will be assured a memorable meal, without losing any sleep.

HINT: If desired, garnish the plate with fresh parsley—it adds a nice touch and a bit of color.

Never Fail Steak
20-25 minutes preparation and cooking time

4 steaks, filet mignon or T-bones, about 1" thick	1/2 cup dry red wine
Salt and black pepper	1 teaspoon Dijon mustard
1/2 cup beef broth	6 black peppercorns

Preheat broiler and move rack so that steaks will be approximately 2" from heat source. Season both sides of steak with salt and pepper. For medium rare meat, broil steaks 8 minutes on one side, turn over and broil for an additional 6 minutes*. While the steaks are cooking, combine beef broth, red wine, Dijon mustard and peppercorns in a small sauce pan. Bring mixture to a boil, reduce heat and simmer until mixture reduces slightly (or until steaks are ready to serve). Remove peppercorns before serving with steak.

*For rare meat, broil 6 minutes on the first side and 5 minutes after turning. For well done meat, broil 11 minutes on the first side and 9 minutes after turning.

NOTE: If you are cooking steaks on an outdoor grill, reduce times by 1-2 minutes for each side.

Oven Baked Tomatoes

10-15 minutes to prepare   *20-25 minutes to bake*

3-4	medium ripe tomatoes	2	dashes Tabasco or other hot sauce
1	tablespoon butter or margarine	2	tablespoons Parmesan cheese
1	medium onion, chopped	2	tablespoons fresh parsley, minced
1	packed tablespoon brown sugar		Salt and black pepper to taste

Preheat oven to 375 degrees. Cut tomatoes in half and remove the core and seeds with a spoon. Cut each half in half and place side by side in a shallow baking dish. In a small sauce pan, saute onion in butter over low heat until tender. Add brown sugar, season with salt and pepper and stir until sugar dissolves. Add Tabasco sauce and mix well. Spoon a teaspoon of onion mixture into each tomato quarter. Sprinkle the top with Parmesan cheese and then parsley. Cover dish with foil and bake for 20-25 minutes or until tomatoes are soft. Serve immediately.

Red Potatoes and Garlic

10 minutes to prepare   *35-40 minutes to bake*

8-10	small new red potatoes
1/4	cup butter
2	cloves garlic, minced
1/2	teaspoon salt
1/4	teaspoon black pepper

Preheat oven to 375 degrees (these can be baked with the tomatoes, just add 5 minutes to the cooking time). Wash the potatoes and remove any black knots. Slice potatoes in half lengthwise and chop into 1" chunks. Melt butter in a small sauce pan or in the microwave and add garlic, salt and pepper. Dip potato slices into butter mixture, turn to coat all sides, and place on an ungreased baking sheet. Bake for 35-40 minutes, or until potatoes are tender and golden brown. Serve.

Creamy Cheesecake

NOTE: This cake can, and should, be prepared up to one day in advance and refrigerated.

20-25 minutes to prepare   *1 hour to bake*   *(Allow extra time for cooling)*

1 1/2	cups crushed vanilla wafers (crush in food processor or blender)
6	tablespoons honey
2 1/4	lbs. cream cheese
1 1/4	cups granulated sugar
4	large eggs
6	tablespoons all-purposed flour
1 1/2	cups sour cream
1	teaspoon vanilla extract
1/4	cup confectioners sugar
1	teaspoon cinnamon

Preheat oven to 325 degrees. Combine vanilla wafer crumbs and honey and mix well with a fork. Press mixture firmly into the bottom of a lightly greased 10" springform pan and set aside. Beat cream cheese in a large mixing bowl until creamy and smooth. Gradually add sugar and mix well. Add eggs, one at a time, mixing well after each addition. Gradually add flour and mix on low speed until blended. Add sour cream and vanilla and mix until just blended, being careful not to overmix because an overmixed cheesecake will crack during cooking. Pour mixture into springform pan and bake for 1 hour. Turn oven off, open door and allow cake to cool in oven for 1 hour. Remove cheesecake from oven and cool thoroughly in refrigerator. When ready to serve, combine confectioners sugar and cinnamon in a small bowl. Pour mixture into a sifter and sift a generous amount on top of cake. Serve with fresh fruit as garnish if desired.

SPICE INDEX

ALLSPICE - aroma and flavor of cinnamon, nutmeg and cloves, sweet and warm

Commonly used in: pot roast, poached fish, meat marinades, stew, vinegar, preserved fruits, pickles, vegetables, cakes spiced breads, cookies, fruit pies, meat loaf, spaghetti sauce, barbecue sauce, salad dressings, sweet potatoes, squash, graham cracker pie crust

ANISE - licorice-like flavor and aroma

Commonly used in: breads, cakes, pastries, candies, fish

BASIL -the most common, store-bought variety of basil is sweet. Aromatic, sweet, fresh, fragrant, mint-like flavor and aroma. (Using fresh is best when possible)

Commonly used in: pesto, soups, omelettes, fish, vegetables (basil has an astounding affinity with tomatoes, and tastes great with eggplant, zucchini and bell peppers), shrimp, rice and pasta dishes. NOTE: Add to hot dishes just before serving so the flavor isn't lost during long cooking times.

BAY LEAVES - bitter, pungent

Commonly used in: soups, stews, stocks, marinades for beef and lamb, tomato dishes, pot roasts, add to boiling water for poached fish, corned beef, ham dishes. NOTE: Use sparingly.

BOUQUET GARNI - herbs tied together in cheese cloth for use in stocks, soups and stews to enhance flavor. Usually made up of parsley, thyme and bay leaf (other spices may be added).

CARAWAY - similar flavor to licorice (commonly found in rye breads)

Commonly used in: fruit dishes, cakes, breads

CARDAMON - member of the ginger family, strong lemony taste

Commonly used in: Indian dishes

CAYENNE PEPPER - very hot, pungent, savory taste and bitter aroma

Commonly used in: fish, shellfish, cheese and egg dishes, chicken salads, soup, chili, spaghetti sauce

CELERY SALT - blend of ground celery seed and coarsely ground salt

Commonly used in: tomato juice, fish and chicken dishes, cauliflower, potato salad, macaroni salad, stuffed eggs

CELERY SEED - intensifies the flavor of celery

Commonly used in: soups, stews, breads, tomato juice

CHERVIL - member of the parsley family, delicate, sweet taste, sweeter and more fragrant than parsley

Commonly used in: sauces, soups, egg dishes (i.e., scrambled, omelettes, quiches), bearnaise sauce, avocado dip, mild cheese spreads, steak or roast beef (added just before serving), rice, pasta (added with butter or oil). NOTE: Chervil is best used fresh and it is recommended that it be added to a hot meal just before serving, so as not to lose the flavor.

CHILES - chili peppers

Commonly used in: stews, vegetables, meat, fish, sauces, pickles, salads

CHILI POWDER - a staple in Mexican dishes; blend of chili peppers, cumin, oregano, salt and garlic

Commonly used in: Mexican dishes, chili con carne, shellfish, cocktail sauces for fish, boiled and scrambled eggs, gravies, stews, hamburgers

CHIVES - delicate onion flavor

Commonly used in: garnishes, sauces, soups, salads, scrambled eggs, vegetables

CILANTRO (fresh)/**CORIANDER** (dried)

Commonly used in: Fresh cilantro in fish and meat dishes. Coriander seeds in fish, sausage, breads, cakes, roasted meat, and with dishes using curry.

CINNAMON - aromatic, derivative of bark

Commonly used in: baked goods, sweet potatoes, cakes, cookies, fruit dishes, custards, puddings, fruited breads, desserts, apple sauce

CLOVES - (whole or ground) dried flower bud of a tropical tree

Commonly used in: stews, sauces, gravies, stocks, apple dishes, gingerbread, baked ham, pickled and stewed fruits, tomato juice, spiced sweet syrup, pot roast, meat marinades, breads, cakes, cookies, tapioca, pumpkin, apple and mince pies, rice and chocolate puddings, sweet potatoes, bean, pork roast, meat loaf, corned beef, roast beef, chicken, baked fish

CREAM OF TARTAR - white crystalline form of salt

Commonly used in: to prevent sugar from crystallizing in the preparation of candies, frostings and sweet desserts. Also controls the rise of dough in baking.

CUMIN - pungent flavor and aroma, from the carrot family

Commonly used in: curry dishes, Mexican dishes, scrambled eggs, omelettes, shish kebabs, meat loaf, hash, veal, chili con carne

CURRY POWDER - spicy, aromatic, made of several pungent spices

Commonly used in: chili con carne, stews, cream sauces, lamb, beef, shrimp, chicken and rice dishes, fruit compote, dips

DILL - a sweeter, more aromatic leaf than parsley, fresh bouquet flavor

Commonly used in: Fresh or dry dill weed (leaf of the dill plant) used in soups, salads, sauces, seafood, vegetables and egg dishes. Use dill seeds in soups, stews, cheese and egg dishes, pickled gherkins.

FENNEL - carrot family, strong taste of anise

Commonly used in: pork, veal, soups, salads, fish

GARLIC POWDER - use in place of fresh garlic; 1/8 teaspoon equals 1 clove of fresh garlic

Commonly used in: Italian dishes, vegetable dishes such as green beans, zucchini, eggplant, yellow squash, carrots, stewed tomatoes, meat dishes such as pork, lamb or beef, used in tomato, barbecue and spaghetti sauces, vegetable, minestrone and lentil soup, chicken casseroles, pot pies, beef or lamb stew, pot roast or braised beef, marinades, garlic bread

GINGER - hot, spicy-sweet flavor

Commonly used in: breads, cakes, cookies, sweet sauces, custards, Chinese dishes, gingerbread, pumpkin and apple pie, stewed fruit, carrots, sweet potatoes, pork, chicken, beef

JUNIPER - of the pine tree family

Commonly used in: game meats, stuffing, sauces, pates, pork, chicken, meat stews

LEMON PEEL - thinly pared outer rind of mature tree-ripened lemons that is dried and milled

Commonly used in: use in place of fresh lemon peel in breads, cakes cookies, custards, sauces, sprinkled over peas, carrots, and used in cream sauces for chicken, lamb and pork

LEMON PEPPER - citrus flavored seasoning made from pure table salt, coarse black pepper, citric acid, red and green bell peppers, garlic, onion and lemon flavor

Commonly used in: either sprinkled on roasted or baked dishes or used in basting gravy for meat and poultry, salad dressing

MACE - derived from the same fruit as nutmeg

Commonly used in: stews, sweet dishes, cakes, sauces, fish, veal, chicken, vegetables, whipped cream, doughnuts, preserved fruits, fruit salads, spinach, potatoes, carrots, meat stuffing, especially good with chocolate desserts, puddings, gingerbread, pound cake, fruit cakes and pies, custard

MARJORAM (French) - Mild flavor of oregano, with a sweet taste

Commonly used in: stews, meat sauce, egg dishes, poultry, roasts, gravies, bean soup, pork chops, roast lamb, dressings, many Italian dishes, often used with thyme and in salads (tastes great on all green vegetables). NOTE: Best added at the end of cooking time, for recipes that have long cooking times, to prevent the spice from losing flavor.

MINT - Cool refreshing menthol flavor and aroma

Commonly used in: desserts, jelly, lamb

MUSTARD - pungent taste, comes in seeds or yellow powder (ground seeds)

Commonly used in: chicken, turkey, roast beef, ham, roast pork, Newburg or cheese sauce, seafood, deviled crab, salad dressing, vegetables (especially cabbage, celery, asparagus, baked beans, broccoli, potatoes), egg dishes, Welsh rarebit, cocktail and barbecue sauces, cream soups

NUTMEG - aromatic, seeds derived from an evergreen native to Indonesia

Commonly used in: puddings, pancakes, carrots, spinach, asparagus, sweet potatoes, mushroom soup, creamed chicken, lamb, sausage, banana and zucchini breads, spice cake, fruit cake, cookies, stewed fruit, sprinkled over eggnog

OREGANO - strong odor, pungent flavor, mint-like

Commonly used in: Italian dishes, pizza, meat, fish, vegetables (has a strong affinity with green beans), tomato juice, barbecue sauce, egg and cheese dishes, seafood salads, stuffing, sauces

PAPRIKA (most commonly Hungarian in the market)-made from dried and ground red peppers

Commonly used in: stews, soups, vegetables, broiled and roasted meats, ragouts, meat pies, Hungarian goulash, chicken, fish, as a garnish sprinkled over egg and cheese dishes, deviled eggs and cream sauces

PARSLEY - extremely versatile seasoning and/or garnish, brings out natural flavor of other herbs

Commonly used in: soups, salads, meat, fish, poultry, sauces, gravies, dressings, virtually all vegetable dishes, butter sauces

POPPY SEEDS - nutty taste

Commonly used in: sweet dishes, cakes, strudel fillings, sprinkled on breads and rolls before baking

POULTRY SEASONING - blend of thyme, sage, marjoram, rosemary, black pepper and nutmeg

Commonly used in: stuffing for poultry, veal and lamb, casseroles, barbecue sauce, meat loaf, herb bread

ROSEMARY - sweet, pungent, floral

Commonly used in: roasted meat and poultry, breads, potatoes, stews, soups

SAFFRON - slightly bitter taste, used to color and flavor foods

Commonly used in: bouillabaisse, fish, shellfish, sauces, rice dishes, soups, cakes

SAGE - powerful, pungent, camphor aroma and flavor

Commonly used in: Italian dishes, pasta sauces

SAVORY - hot and peppery version of thyme

Commonly used in: beans, peas, fish (especially trout), sauces and meats

SEASONED SALT - blend of salt, herbs and spices

Commonly used in: to enhance the flavor of meats, soups, gravies, stews, casseroles. Also used in barbecuing, and sprinkled on salads, poultry, vegetables and eggs.

SESAME SEEDS - rich, nutty taste (used raw and toasted)

Commonly used in: sprinkled on breads and rolls before baking, toasted and sprinkled over vegetables, noodles, dips, mixed with butter for fish and vegetables

TARRAGON - pungent, anise flavor

Commonly used in: meat gravies, sauces, salads, roasted meats, aspics, mushroom soup, lobster, deviled eggs, French and Russian dressing, tomato juice, egg dishes, cream sauces, chicken, fish, pickles, vinegar

Leaves can be crumbled and added to salads and vegetable dishes.

THYME - member of the mint family, aromatic, pungent flavor

Commonly used in: stocks, soups, vegetables (especially tomatoes, potatoes, green beans and bell peppers), poultry, grilled and roasted beef dishes, cheese spreads, broiled, baked or fried fish, cream sauce for onions

TURMERIC - member of the ginger family, fragrant, curry-like, bitter

Commonly used in: coloring agent for curries, pickles, rice dishes, drinks and sweet dishes

VANILLA EXTRACT - sweet, aromatic, flavorful

Commonly used in: chocolate, ice cream, cakes, cookies, meringues, cream desserts, custards, rice pudding, souffles, mousses

TERMINOLOGY

BLANCHE - to immerse into rapidly boiling water for a short period of time. This procedure is frequently used with vegetables to tenderize and assure color retention. Commonly proceeded by further cooking of a different method.

BRAISE - to cook slowly in a covered pot, using steam as method of heating and tenderizing

CLARIFY - as in clarifying butter, to heat over very low heat to allow butter to melt and separate; clarified portion is yellow liquid between white foam and residue on the bottom of pan

DEGLAZE - takes place in a pan that has been used for sauteing or pan frying; procedure where liquid is added to pan, cooking juices and brown bits are scraped up from the bottom and incorporated into the liquid and the mixture is then reduced to a thick syrup to be made into a sauce

DICE - to cut into small cubes

GLAZE - liquid dripped over food surface (i.e., breads, cakes) that becomes hard and glossy. Usually made from a combination of confectioners sugar and fruit juice.

HEAPING - to fill above the full line in the shape of a mound

JULIENNE - cut into thin strips

MINCE - to cut or chop into very small bits

PARBOIL - to boil briefly in lightly salted water before further cooking of another method

PARE - to peel off skin

POACH - to cook in a small amount of simmering liquid

SAUTE - to fry in a small amount of shortening

SCALD - to bring to a temperature slightly below the boiling point

SEAR - to brown quickly over very high heat to seal in juices in tougher cuts of meat; browning also adds flavor and a crisp texture

SIMMER - to keep at a temperature just below the rapid boiling point

SLICE - to cut a thin flat piece or wedge

NOTES

1. When making dough, yeast is activated by mixing with lukewarm water or milk. The yeast should dissolve within five minutes. If it does not dissolve, or if it becomes lumpy, toss it and start over. The dough will not rise if the yeast is not activated.

2. When making tarts and pastries use corn oil. Tarts made with regular vegetable or other oil taste exactly like the oil!

3. When preparing and kneading dough, be certain dough is not too sticky. If dough sticks to sides of bowl or counter-top, add more flour as necessary—and always flour and reflour your work surface. Trying to scrape dough off a counter is not a fun task.

4. Recipes that call for milk usually assume that you will be using whole milk. When low-fat or skim milk is substituted, the cooking time may change. Be sure to keep this in mind when baking.

5. Strawberries should be bought the same day you use them (or within a couple of days). Never buy unripened strawberries because they do not ripen once they have been picked.

6. Sifted confectioners sugar can be a great way to hide ugly mistakes in dessert dishes. In addition, it can be used to enhance bland tasting desserts and treats.

7. Homemade muffins do not keep fresh for more than a few days. If you must make them in advance, freeze them. Homemade muffins become moldy very quickly because they do not contain preservatives.

8. Corn oil tastes best in baked goods - and it's one of the better oils to use if you are watching your cholesterol intake.

9. Raspberries should never be washed. If necessary, rinse under slow running, cold tap water before using or eating.

10. When a recipe calls for warm tortillas (i.e., fajitas, enchiladas, etc.) to prevent drying out, brush melted butter between tortillas before heating. If you don't like to use a lot of butter, the stoneware cookers work very well, using water and steam as a means to prevent drying out. Tortillas can also be warmed, one at a time, by placing directly on a warm gas or electric stove top for a brief period of time.

11. In most recipes that call for oil (except in this book), with the exception of baked goods, the amount of oil can be decreased.

12. New red potatoes perform better in most types of potato salad. The regular baking potatoes turn to mashed potatoes when stirred.

13. When saving cooked pasta, add a touch of olive or vegetable oil before refrigerating to keep it moist and prevent sticking.

14. When grilling onions on a barbecue grill, put them on the skewer first, then cut them - this prevents them from falling apart.

15. Apple dishes tastes best when made with Mackintosh apples.

16. If you don't have a rolling pin yet, use a bottle of wine!

17. When melting butter with flour, as a thickener in sauces, the butter should be melted first. The flour should then be added gradually, while constantly mixing with a wire whisk. The mixture should be cooked over low heat for about 3-5 minutes, until smooth - otherwise whatever liquid is added will undoubtedly get lumpy.

18. Corn starch mixed with milk (for Custard) must be thoroughly mixed to a thick consistency before being added to the rest of the ingredients. If it's not, it will either curdle or never thicken to the correct consistency.

19. When buying extra lean meat, don't be alarmed if you notice a bit of browning on the sides of the meat. Because the meat is extra lean, it does not breath as well, thus causing browning. Lightly brown meat is still safe to eat.

20. When a recipe calls for ground cloves, and you only have whole cloves, pinch the top portion of the clove between two fingers and work it until it's fine.

21. In most of my recipes, where applicable, I have given you the option of using butter or margarine. If the recipe does **not** give you the option, I suggest using the one indicated. In some cases, there is a definite difference and you will achieve the better result by using the one suggested.

22. When a recipe tells you to "sift together the dry ingredients" (ie., flour, baking soda, salt, etc.) put the flour in the sifter first, followed by the remaining ingredients. All other ingredients should be added close to the center of the sifter before sifting, because the center goes down first, enabling you to effectively combine all ingredients.

23. When rolling out dough, for pie crusts, etc., place dough between two pieces of wax paper. This prevents the mess caused by a floured surface and makes the entire process much easier.

24. When making cookies in advance, store already baked cookies in an air tight container with a slice of bread. The cookies will absorb the moisture from the bread and stay moist and fresh.

25. Poaching eggs - fill a small sauce pan with water and a pinch of salt. Bring to a vigorous boil. Turn heat down until water is simmering. Crack each egg into a small bowl (I do this in advance to be sure that the yolk doesn't run). Pour egg into center of pan and turn heat down until water is still. Let egg cook 2-3 minutes, depending on desired doneness. Remove with a slotted spoon and dab bottom of spoon with a paper towel.

26.   To alleviate the extra fat and calories that greasing a muffin pan can cause, use muffin liners (it also aids in cleanup!).

27.   Once batter for muffins is prepared, never let it stand for long before baking. The leavening agents in the batter react quickly once combined, therefore they need to be baked immediately.

28.   Use fresh herbs whenever possible in recipes that call for it. They create a more dynamic flavor. However, dried herbs can and should be used in soups and stews because fresh become wilted and discolored.

29.   Blanching vegetables - this is done to preserve the color and flavor of fresh vegetables. Many times, blanching is be followed by a different method of further cooking. To blanch vegetables, immerse them into a large pot of boiling water, return to boil and cook for 1-3 minutes (depending on the vegetable). Drain in colander and immerse under very cold water to prevent further cooking.

30.   If you are unsure what part of the broccoli to use, use it all. Start by cutting off the florets (the flowery portion), leaving the small, thin stalk attached. Trim off any leaves. To the remaining thick stalk, peel off the outer layer with a sharp knife or peeler (the thick outer layer of the stalk is coarse and unpleasant tasting). Cut broccoli into desired pieces and cook as directed in recipe.

31.   For the best tasting and most crispy salad, choose your favorite fresh greens; Boston, Romaine, red and green leaf lettuces, etc. For best results, tear the lettuce leaves into bite size pieces before washing. Wash under cold water to remove dirt and sand, and drain in a colander or salad spinner. Wrap in a dry paper towel and refrigerate for 5 minutes before serving (do not serve too chilled, or the lettuce will be tasteless). Serve with your favorite dressing and fresh vegetables.

32. When cooking pasta, depending on the dish, it should be cooked, drained, immersed under water and drained again. If you are serving the pasta immediately, immerse under HOT water to remove the starch. If you are not serving pasta immediately, immerse under COLD water to prevent further cooking.

33. For hard boiled eggs, bring a large pot of water to a boil. Gently place eggs in water and return to boil. Reduce heat slightly and boil for exactly 14 minutes (the water may be just under the boiling point). Remove eggs from water and immerse in very cold water. Peel shell when eggs are cooled.

34. To scald milk, heat it in a saucepan until tiny bubbles appear around the edges of the pan. Scalding is just below the boiling point, so do not let the milk come to a boil.

35. To get more juice out of a lemon, roll in on a hard surface with the palm of your hand before squeezing.

36. White pepper is stronger than black pepper. When substituting, use half the amount of white as you would black.

INDEX

Please accept this opportunity to share this "Great Book" with a friend or family member. You will give great pleasures to all! Also, we have a few other special books for those who love to cook.

"This For That: A Treasury of Savvy Substitutions for the Creative Cook" by Meryl Nelson

Hints, Recipes, How-To's for using THIS when you're out of THAT, includes microwave directions. As seen in *Family Circle* and many great magazines and newspapers. Don't be without one!

$6.95   #847

❖ ❖ ❖ ❖ ❖ ❖ ❖ ❖ ❖ ❖ ❖ ❖ ❖ ❖ ❖ ❖

"The Newlywed Cookbook" by Robin Walsh

What a lovely gift for the newlyweds in your life. The Famous *Chef Tell* says, "Amusing, creative ideas for the beginner cook. I highly recommend it!"

"With these recipes and food preparation tips, you won't need to phone mom to cook great meals!" Cele G. Lalli
Editor-In-Chief, *Modern Bride*

$12.95   #877

❖ ❖ ❖ ❖ ❖ ❖ ❖ ❖ ❖ ❖ ❖ ❖ ❖ ❖ ❖ ❖

Kids Love To Cook

So how about teaching them with "Learning Through Cooking: A Cooking Program for Children Two to Ten" by Nancy Ferreira. They will learn many important things with this GREAT little book.
$7.95   #658

Please accept this opportunity to share this "Great Book" with a friend or family member. You will give great pleasures to all! Also, we have a few other special books for those who love to cook.

"This For That: A Treasury of Savvy Substitutions for the Creative Cook" by Meryl Nelson

Hints, Recipes, How-To's for using THIS when you're out of THAT, includes microwave directions. As seen in *Family Circle* and many great magazines and newspapers. Don't be without one!

$6.95   #847

❖ ❖ ❖ ❖ ❖ ❖ ❖ ❖ ❖ ❖ ❖ ❖ ❖ ❖ ❖ ❖ ❖

"The Newlywed Cookbook" by Robin Walsh

What a lovely gift for the newlyweds in your life. The Famous *Chef Tell* says, "Amusing, creative ideas for the beginner cook. I highly recommend it!"

"With these recipes and food preparation tips, you won't need to phone mom to cook great meals!" Cele G. Lalli
Editor-In-Chief, *Modern Bride*

$12.95   #877

❖ ❖ ❖ ❖ ❖ ❖ ❖ ❖ ❖ ❖ ❖ ❖ ❖ ❖ ❖ ❖ ❖

Kids Love To Cook

So how about teaching them with "Learning Through Cooking: A Cooking Program for Children Two to Ten" by Nancy Ferreira. They will learn many important things with this GREAT little book.
$7.95   #658

About the Author

Robin Walsh, an avid cook, has written *The Newlywed Cookbook* for those who wish to create sensational meals for two, as well as create great meals for their guests. Her desire to learn more about food and cooking began soon after marriage when she tried to prepare wonderful (and edible) meals. Unfortunately, take-out pizza seemed to be the dinner of choice after many catastrophes in the kitchen. Recognizing the need for a basic cookbook for beginners, she began to compile a wealth of information using first hand experiences. She shares many of her experiences with food and cooking—both successes and failures. She plans to continue experimenting in the kitchen and she hopes that other newlyweds will benefit by reading her book and experimenting as well.

As in-house food and nutrition consultant for Family Circle magazine, Robin developed stories and she created, tested, and edited recipes. Her features appeared in dozens of issues and included topics such as: "Lowfat Cooking"; "What's for dinner?"; and "Holiday Eating Guide." She wrote a feature article on how Bill Clinton could cut the fat out of his diet, and she also wrote a chapter on nutrition in Family Circle's latest cookbook, "The Cook's Book." She has had significant media exposure, appearing on several national television shows, including: CBS This Morning, NBC Today Show, ABC News, Fox News, QVC Network, Montel Williams, and The Television Food Network. Segments included live interviews, on-air cooking demonstrations, nutrition education, and "question and answer" sessions with both the host and the audience.

As freelance food consultant, Robin has written feature articles for Women's Day magazine, Weight Watchers Food Company, and Braun, Inc. She was retained by Weight Watchers to serve as national spokesperson in print and on television for their "Lose 10 lbs. America" promotion.

As cookbook author of *The Newlywed Cookbook* (1990 and 1994 editions), Robin traveled extensively throughout the United States to promote her book. She was interviewed on several radio shows that included callers' questions and comments. She spent two years making in-store public appearances in small towns and large cities, signing books, conducting cooking demonstrations, and providing nutrition information. In the larger arenas, she had the opportunity to work in front of a sizable audience. In smaller towns, she worked one-on-one with consumers, answering questions, providing advice, and discussing the role of nutrition in a healthy lifestyle.

Photographer: John Tuckerman